One Less Bitter Actor

One Less Bitter Actor

An Actor's Survival Guide

Markus Flanagan

SENTIENT PUBLICATIONS

First Sentient Publications edition 2008

A paperback original

Cover design by Kim Johansen, Black Dog Design
Book design by Nicholas Cummings

Library of Congress Cataloging-in-Publication Data

Flanagan, Markus, 1964-
One less bitter actor / by Markus Flanagan.—1st Sentient Publications ed.
p. cm.
ISBN 978-1-59181-063-6
1. Acting—Vocational guidance. I. Title.

PN2055.F55 2007
792.02'8'023—dc22

2007020480

Printed in the United States of America

10 9 8 7 6 5 4 3 2 1

SENTIENT PUBLICATIONS
A Limited Liability Company
1113 Spruce Street
Boulder, CO 80302
www.sentientpublications.com

To the lovely women in my life who make it so damn fun—Brianna, Isabel, Leila, and Gina.

Acknowledgements

Warm thanks to those who helped me with the work on this book: Connie Shaw, Jennifer Palais, Steven Frank, Linda Foster, Marilyn Paige, Mary Anne Perez, Carol Burnett, Keli Lee, Ellie Kanner, Larry Poindexter, and Bert Rotundo.

And a heartfelt hug to the people who mentored, encouraged and inspired me to take that leap and sit down and write: John Bishop, Janet Dulin Jones, Ron Hoffman, Erik King, Adam Chapnick, Marilyn Paige, Stuart Rodgers, Bill Caswell, and Mom and Dad.

Contents

Preface

THIS BOOK IS GEARED TOWARD the career actor—the actor who has made the decision to pursue this endeavor and seeks a place among the working. Since this is not a how-to book or an instant success guide, I don't discuss acting technique. I seek to help those of you who want to shorten your learning curve about how things really work in the acting trade.

I graduated from my acting program and spent many of the following years in what I now call creative suffering, which means many things. At first it meant that I thought everyone was on the same page I was on, and that we all wanted to put out the best product possible. I thought that being the best actor would always get me the job, regardless of how the non-acting elements of an audition went. If I was the most talented, I would get the job. I had no concept that this belief was mine and mine only, and at times it was the very thing that was shooting my career in the foot.

You can learn from my mistakes and my experience, and take my advice on how to read between the lines. Some techniques will be discussed, but this is more of a mental primer for your long term career view. Training is very important, but that's up to you.

You who are fresh out of class or college and find yourself ready for a full attack on "the biz" should find this book a source of encouragement, comfort, and reference. Those of you who are already pursuing this career but wonder if you're missing something should find that this book fills those uneasy gaps between what you imagine your career should be and what's really happening. I'm convinced the creative suffering of my early days slowly sapped from me not only the desire to do my best work, but also my ability. I am writing this book to demystify the process so that you can better understand what we have all come to call rejection. Bitterness appears to be built in to the process, but it doesn't have to be. With a conscious, clear understanding of the days ahead, you will not only enjoy the journey, but you'll put yourself in a position to do your best work.

This book is the distillation of twenty years of experience and what feels like a million "no's" and a million moments of panicked insecurity. The business side of show business embitters the best of us at some point. Let me save you from yourself.

The Beginning

Less Bitterness Through Better Understanding

ALMOST ALL OF THIS PROCESS is mental, perceptual. I'm going to start with the mental picture because I think it's the most important part of this book. Consider this the advice of many actors saying, "If I had known *then*, what I know *now*..."

First, let me dispel a few myths. "Auditions are about finding the best actor for the job." Get that out of your head.

And conversely, "I didn't get the job, so I must not have been good." Very, very wrong—get that out of your head immediately!

Now a truth: Honesty is the most feared and revered quality in Hollywood.

When You Start Out

You will spend a lot of time trying to get the job. But let's talk about why. Why do we need the job so badly? We automatically assume it is the most important part of the whole process, right? Everything we study for and spend our days striving for is about landing the job. Without the job we're just acting alone in our basements, right? Well, the common thinking is we want the job for the money and fame. We can all agree that there's no greater feeling than being paid and admired for doing what you love. After all, this is America, and money is freedom. Fame brings access to places and people that we'd never otherwise encounter. Our lives will simply become more fun and fabulous with an influx of money and fame. This is the conventional thinking, isn't it?

Now, let me inject another possibility for you to consider.

You want the job for the validation—validation of your talent, validation of your ego, and validation that your decision to dedicate your life to this discipline was the right one. Validation of "your artist"—that striving, inspired force to create that lives within you—is your real payoff in getting the job.

Even those of you who have "*always* known you'd be an actor!" still need to know that you are here for the right reason. No matter how good we feel about ourselves, our training, our preparedness, and our looks, there is always self doubt. What better way to tame that vast emptiness of self doubt for a moment than by getting a job? That *must* mean you're right, good, pretty, talented, strong, handsome, and dedicated. If the smart guys and gals that auditioned you think you are good enough to hire, then you *must* be good, etc. You don't have to doubt yourself, because they don't. We all know producers pay only people that they truly believe in, right?

Let's look more deeply at "I want the money."

The money is a great bonus, but our journey into this acting abyss is more about building our self esteem and confidence, one positive comment or one job at a time. You act because you want to express and contribute. You want to influence and indulge. Actors work from their feelings, and don't we all want our feelings validated? It's human nature. No one takes on this career purely for the money. Every actor has a need to show off. It's what makes actors stand up and civilians stay seated.

So consider that idea. Consider that what you're really after is the confirmation of your artist, disguised as the want of money. Isn't that what the Oscars are? A night where the biggest stars get their acting choices confirmed as "the best" that year. Everyone needs the validation, even the best of us.

"Hold on, I'm not ashamed to say I want the fame."

The fame issue is the same. If everyone on the street stops you to say how much he or she loves your work, isn't that validation again? If it were purely about the money, you'd go into something with a higher success-to-rejection ratio.

I present this early in the book, because of the damage that can be done by the belief that getting jobs confirms that you are good, right, talented, etc., and that therefore *not* getting jobs *must* mean that you're *not* good, right, and talented, and that you're clearly on the wrong career path. This battle of winners and losers, something that is pounded into us our whole lives, obscures the reality of our particular situation. It serves to destroy our egos, but it's hardly the truth of the situation. The truth is that actors get jobs for reasons so varied that you do your talent a disservice to accept those reasons as your only source of validation.

In our society we have been trained to know success only by its spoils, but often the best actor for the job isn't the one chosen. More importantly, by accepting the premise that the *only* measure of your value as an actor is whether or not you get the job, you are giving your power and self worth away to others. This is a subjective business. There are no devices to measure talent, there are only opinions. Do yourself a favor. Get in the habit of judging your value by what you know you're capable of. Don't judge yourself by the opinions of others. This new habit will help you avoid three big traps that kill inspiration.

Trap #1

In order to get the job, you will try anything. Using the job as the sole evidence that you belong in the club of great artists will lead you down a path of ignoring your own instincts and second guessing "what they want." Often it's at this very point that we lose touch with what made us want to act in the first place. In the push to land the part, it's easy to abandon the only real value you bring to the room—your individuality.

The trap is real and very easy to fall into. I hope to plant in your mind now the idea that the job is not the prize if you want to create a mindset for the long haul. The job is the temporary prize, something that will pay you to grow and get better. The growth of your artist is the real prize. Think of it this way: if you get the job, you are being paid to learn. If you don't, you are still learning.

Getting a job doesn't instantly make you a better actor. Doing the job well might. But haven't we all looked at someone who got the big role and thought, "What makes him better than me?" The answer might be: nothing. A job just makes getting better more comfortable.

Trap #2

You may be saying to yourself, "But the star-making job *is* the prize because it could set me up for the rest of my career! Make everything easier!" That's true. But let's continue the thought. What is it setting you up for? Is it to be a big enough star to do the work you want? Is it to put yourself in the company of fellow artists you respect? In other words, it is to grow and become a better actor? More famous doesn't mean better. The trap that we actors fall into is thinking that money and fame translate into fulfillment and happiness. We think that landing enough jobs will cure us of feeling inadequate, and all our self doubt will be gone. I'm telling you that getting the job doesn't make you feel secure about anything but your bank account. Complacency isn't part of being an artist.

Trap #3

How many of you have had the thought that you'll do what *they* want until you make it and then you'll be free to do what *you* want? Do you really think any big star is free to play whatever role they want? Don't think for a second that big stars are exempt from the same disappointments and hassles that you experience. They surely have the cushion of money, but when a good role comes up, only one person can play it. They too deal with the same stuff, but on a larger scale. It doesn't become a cakewalk just because you've "made it."

The Opposite of Validation: Rejection

Getting jobs is also the number one way to avoid feeling any more rejection, right? Hasn't absolutely everyone taken the time to tell us that one bullet-proof rule of acting? "You must accept rejection as a way of life." We are indoctrinated with the idea that it's our job to eat dirt for years. It makes sense then that we'd spend a lot of our time trying to avoid rejection.

I'm going to salve the wounds of rejection. I'm doing this early in this book because I'm trying to effect a perspective shift in you. No one—neither acting teachers or other actors—will tell you what I'm about to tell you. The reason rejection hurts so much is that we've been told for so long it's supposed to. It hurts because we've been offered only the view that every "no" is a wholesale rejection of our talent, our looks, our feelings, our ethnic background, and so on. That's scary, hurtful stuff. But the rejection is not all that deep. It's not a complete rejection of you as an artist. It just feels that way.

Being able to get up every day and be excited about pursuing your career is about the nearly impossible task of not taking the rejection of your person, personally. Think about that for a second.

Unlike other salespeople, you don't have a product to hide behind when you're selling (auditioning). They can say to themselves that they didn't sell the vacuum cleaner because the customer thought it was no good. But us? We are the product. It stands to reason, then, that you'd take it to heart when someone doesn't hire you. Obviously they thought you were no good.

But I offer you this shift in perspective.

The rejection is not a rejection of you and your talent; it's merely a rejection of that day's choice. The way you interpreted that role, on that day, in that audition—period. It doesn't necessarily indicate any larger picture about your value as an artist. You might be thinking, "Yes, but if I was any good I'd know how to nail the scene and get the job." Okay, if that's true, then why would any huge star had to have auditioned more than once to get where they are now? If this isn't a developmental process that takes place over time, then what you are saying is that you are a completed project waiting for your starring role to be delivered. If it doesn't come, your one shot is lost, and your career is over.

Let's face it, you're not right for everything you get an audition for. You are probably close for a lot of things, but if you simply make a choice about one element of the audition that doesn't suit the director, you won't get the role, and if you respond as you've been taught to up until now, you'll feel rejected. Yes, you are responsible for the choices you make as an actor, but could you not do any scene five different ways? Could you not follow direction and turn a drama into a comedy if you were asked to? To make this process work, you have to make your best choices, do your best work, and allow for the reality that those choices might be rejected.

Actors search for rejection. If they don't get it they reject themselves.

—Charlie Chaplin

I included that quote for the pessimists who are saying right now, "Yes, but if you hear 'no' enough times, you start to believe it!" Ninety-eight percent of the actors in the world are hearing "no" too. Does this make the one person who gets that particular job the *only* good actor on the planet?

Trap Solution

Understanding your involvement in the audition process will take the hurt out of rejection. The difficulty of rejection may still be there, but the hurt will decrease a great deal. This understanding is a powerful tool. If you seek validation solely by accomplishing the work you set out to do in *that* audition, *that* day, in *that* room, you will come to see every audition as another opportunity to grow and get better. It will not feel like the business is punishing you for trying your hardest. Your behavior will always be appropriate. You will avoid the embittered actor syndrome and consequently, you will audition better.

If you keep your eye on the real prize—your personal growth—rejection will become more manageable. Keeping this in mind will save you from the insanity of trying to apply normal, everyday logic and reason to a business that doesn't follow any line of logic or reason. Trust me, days spent trying to figure out "what they want" are long, overwhelming days. Stick to trying to figure out what you want to accomplish with any given acting opportunity.

Earlier in this chapter I wrote that the audition process isn't about finding the best actor for the job. I will explain that assertion in the chapter on auditioning.

Understanding the Other Guys

I want to help you understand "us" and "them." This business is run on two things: fear and perception.

Fear

The people you will be meeting with or auditioning for carry as much fear and insecurity about their positions and abilities as you do. Believe it. They may conceal it better, but they experience it too. Each of them must earn their next job, just like you. Though they do not have to memorize dialogue and create a character, they have other factors to contend with. They create from thin air and can be very troubled by difficult decisions they must make. They constantly try to bridge the gap between art and commerce, for the benefit of commerce.

The decision makers who sit in auditions know very little about what will create a box office hit and what won't. They make their best educated guess. A bad decision could easily cost them their job, their reputation, and their future in the business. It is no wonder they fear making a bad decision. This has resulted in the "no" default system in Hollywood. A "no" will keep you your job a lot longer than a "yes" will. "No's" are easy to give, while a "yes" is a grueling task. These people are human, and they are guessing. If they weren't guessing and they really did know what works, then every movie ever made would be a hit. Networks wouldn't shoot thirty TV pilots to find the two that they put on the air. The President of NBC wouldn't ever say at a press conference, "Last year a lot of our shows, quite frankly, sucked."

These people have been chosen to guess because their guesses, more often than not, are profitable for the company. However, they never really know what the outcome of anything is going to be. Great movies on paper make no money, and odd little risky movies become huge hits. We all know this, so imagine sitting back in a chair watching actors come through and wondering which one will be the hit maker and which one will make it just another nice show. They have to guess, they can't really know.

Now consider how much easier it is for a guesser to choose an actor who isn't guessing about himself. The actor who comes in prepared, composed, and focused on acting for his two minutes makes it infinitely easier for a guesser to lean his way. After all, you have the words, your training, and a desire to act, so what's stopping you from being the best choice that day? I want you to consider how a focused engagement of your skill set helps take away their fear of choosing you. You won't feel their dilemma when you're in the room, because no one in their position ever shows, or even hints at, the fact that they are anything but stone cold sure of themselves. They have to. They're too scared to admit the whole thing is chance. If they make enough decisions, one will pay off. One big hit camouflages ten flops. It's how studios are run. One *Titanic* makes up for the losses on the other tries.

As the young, insecure, beginning artist, you pick up on the practiced confidence of the director or producer or studio executive, and believe that they can really pick the next big talent. If it isn't you, then you can easily walk away thinking that they know more about your talent than you do. He is in charge for a reason, right? He writes the checks, right? He must know, right?

Wrong.

Understand that they get paid to guess. What you're doing is allowing a guess to validate your talent. Doesn't that sound a little too random? Don't you think you know more about your abilities than someone whose job is to guess and hope? By assigning that authority to a guesser you're allowing your two or three minutes in the room with them to either validate or invalidate your years of effort. Remember, art is subjective.

Please consider that everyone is taking their best guess. By and large, these are not hurtful people; they just have very costly decisions to make. They do the best they can, but we've all seen big stars do movies that are unbearable to watch. Do you think the studio executives who green lighted the film sat there before it started and said, "Let's just make a crappy movie this time"? For instance, *The Drew Carey Show* was a bona fide hit TV show, but years before it aired, the same creator shot a pilot with essentially the same layout and theme that failed. An actor named George Clooney was in that pilot. That show should have been a big hit, right? George Clooney is a huge talent. So then why did it take a few years, a stand up comedian named Drew Carey, and a new supporting cast to become a hit? Why didn't it work with George Clooney?

The difference?

Matching the actor's talent to the material is the difference. In this case it was Drew Carey and his supporting cast. No one knows what will work or when, but there are people whose job it is to guess. You will never have to guess if you do your homework, prepare, show up, and do your best work. *Don't ever get into your own guessing game about what they want.* Or for that matter, don't try to predict the outcome based on factors such as how they act toward you, or what time of day your appointment is. You have to stick to the task at hand, and the task is acting, not thinking, your way through your auditions. They will guess and hire an actor. They won't guess and hire a fellow guesser.

Which brings us to our next topic—what helps them make their guess?

Perception

The *perception* that you are the best choice at the time is how they arrive at giving you the job. They never know. They just perceive it, so it becomes a fact. When people are guessing, you'd like to think they have the strength of conviction to guess with their gut. Some decision makers do, but they are in a very small minority. Most guessers go with their perception of who is hot. They bolster their perception with "facts," but it's all perception and guesses. There is no solid ground here. We are not in an arena where results can be measured by a stopwatch. (They do use box office and the Neilson Ratings scale, which itself is a flawed device because all it indicates is what is selling, not why it's selling.) We in the arts live in a world of subjective intellectual properties. There is no way to measure good from bad except by what people think, so we are in a field beholden to opinions. Two like opinions can become a fact; a press release written by the actress herself can become a fact. An article written in almost any magazine or newspaper anywhere can become a fact.

There is a joke that goes like this. A studio executive takes home three scripts to read for the weekend. Monday morning he gets in his office, and he gets a call from an agent asking what he thought of script A. He says, "I don't know, I haven't talked to anyone yet."

Once something is accepted as a fact, it can be traded on. So if you're someone with a $50 million movie at stake, and you read, hear, or overhear that someone said so-and-so is "the best actor in the free world," wouldn't that make your decision to cast so-and-so a little bit easier? You now have some kind of validation that you are choosing the best actor in the free world. You stand less chance of losing your job if you make a choice that's in line with the popular perception. But does anyone really *know* who the best actor is? Every agent, writer, and producer tries to get buzz for his project, client, script. He wants to create the perception of being hot. We have all seen performances that we thought were crap that nevertheless enjoyed rave reviews. We've thought to ourselves, "I guess I missed something, because I thought it stunk." No. We're dealing with a publicist who's creating a perception. They get enough "experts" to say it's a great performance, and suddenly it's accepted that it's a great performance, and thus that actor must be great. A guesser trying to choose the right actor has to feel better about choosing someone whom "everyone" says is great.

Understanding the power and role of that intangible thing called perception is good for two reasons:

1. As a young or new actor in the marketplace you can start to believe someone else's perception of you. It's powerful to hear about the impression you made, but remember, it's just a perception. It's not a fact. If it doesn't jibe with who you think you are, it can quickly kill your inspiration. (Let me be clear. I'm certainly not saying it's good to ignore honest feedback from good sources about how you affect people.) You can start to

feel awkward in your own skin for what you know is being thought about you. It's just ether.

2. Even worse, you can try to mold yourself to the perception that's being bestowed upon a popular working actor of your ilk. The theory "If that's what they want, maybe I too can be that" can be very dangerous to your ego and your talent.

The Newcomer

When you're starting out, you may think you are at zero and have to build the perception of yourself. This is not true. When you walk into the room you're something very valuable—raw potential, fresh and open. Along with that, of course, will be your height, hair color, ethnicity, training, sex appeal, and who your agent is. These are what you bring to the table initially. The biggest attraction is that you are new. You may encounter some resistance to getting a meeting, or getting seen by a casting director, agent, or director, but that's only because of the volume of actors doing the same thing. The reality is that everyone in the business loves the idea of discovering someone new, someone they can take into a casting session and wow their bosses with.

Now, how do you capitalize on this little gift that lasts only a short while? By doing your best work always, always, always. No excuses. Do whatever you have to do to walk in totally prepared and do your best work. Doing bad work in any of those early, and dare I say it, fragile auditions can damage the vitality of the pristine perception you bring in the room. The perception will be that you always show up on time, excited, very prepared, and ready to do your best work. A perception like that is gold, and you can create it.

Don't be intimidated by the perception game. Understand it. The talk, gossip, and advice are constant, ever changing, and not based on anything real anyway. In a business where gossip is a sport, bad news is much more fun to spread than good news, but if all they have is good news of you, gossip becomes your best friend. Always do your best work, and leave gracefully.

Your Perception of Yourself Gets Shaped by the Pros

When you are new to the process, it's easy to accept the power or expertise of those you encounter. But confidence is confidence, and the person who has it, based on the full understanding of his place in the puzzle, will gain the envied perception of strength.

Your talent is never wrong. It can be inappropriate for a particular part, but it can't ever be just plain wrong. Out of habit, the words *right* and *wrong* are always used. "You weren't right for this." "She's all wrong for that part." Hearing right and wrong so often can lead you to think that things are black and white. You're right or you're wrong. Your talent is wrong. Your person is wrong, your beliefs are wrong. Because if they were right, you'd be working—right? Actually no, that's wrong.

It is my contention that these are the elements that begin the death of the inspired artist who's reading this book. So clear your head of right and wrong in that sense. If you did the work and prepared yourself to do the audition, then you were right. You might be wrong for this particular project, but that's all. It's that simple.

Let the guessing game be their problem. Don't add to it.

Please let my words seep in, and understand your power. Your talent, your way of thinking, your appearance, your life experience, your spark of understanding for the character are the exciting things you bring in the room at any time, but especially in the beginning. Don't waste any of your magic on being intimidated by the guessers in the room who will never take the time to remind you that they're praying that your talent will be the perfect match for their project. Believe it or not, there are times when you totally lose sight of the fact that auditions are about finding someone to fill a role.

Less bitterness through better understanding.

NY vs. LA

When you walk into a restaurant in Los Angeles, everyone looks up to see whether you're a celebrity or they should ignore you.

When you walk into a restaurant in New York, everyone ignores you.

There is a very real stereotype attached to each place: "New York has dedicated, well taught, serious actors. LA has lazy, wannabe, pretty people." (And Chicago is loaded with huge talents who go to either coast but remain fiercely loyal to their hometown.)

The truth is that both coasts have their share of wannabes and bad actors as well as dedicated, gifted performers.

The other truth is that most New York actors go to LA to get work. I don't know a single actor in New York who hasn't gone to LA for at least a pilot season, seeking work. Your talent makes you an actor, not your city of residence, but as I said, this is a business of perceptions.

The ridiculousness of the rivalry between the cities is big. Being a New York actor automatically brands you as a struggling, romantic, dark, mad genius. Whereas being an LA actor makes you fancy free, lazy, untrained—a money actor. It's false, but it exists. There are plenty of lazy, bad, New York actors who wear their city like a badge of artistic credibility every day. And there are plenty of LA time-killers who claim to be actors simply because they are waiters. If you are a New York actor, don't perpetuate this stupid division. It just points out your insecurity. If you're an LA actor, don't feel you're missing something by not having trained or lived in New York.

The acting trade is a large collector for people who really don't have a career plan. Since so many actors are unemployed (as actors) so much of the time, one can still be considered part of the rank and file of the acting trade without ever getting an acting job. It connects you with a community of artists, and that's attractive to a lot of folks who are searching for their next move in life. New York, by virtue of the fact that it's just a harder place to live, attracts less of this type of person. You are made to decide faster how you're going to live your life, so I will say there is often more dedication and discipline to the New York actor. Time is expensive there, so unless you're very wealthy, finding-yourself time is tough to come by. You dedicate yourself to your goals more quickly.

LA has the ease of day-to-day living that affords people the comfort to take their time. The weather is very agreeable, distractions plentiful, and most importantly, living spaces are nicer. The rents for small, dark, edgy apartments are outrageous in New York. But those crappy places make you decide what you want to be when you grow up faster than in LA. There's truth to the saying "if you can make it there... ." The summer heat in New York is brutal, and winter is hard as well, but you do get four seasons. LA has two seasons—summer and rain.

LA really is a one-industry town, and you are dependent on a car for commuting. So if you don't seek out a diversity of lifestyles, it's easy to become isolated by your influences. In New York there are many other major industries, so there is much more diversity in the population, and since the city is based on public transportation, that diversity finds you. Unless you are a shut-in you have no choice but to be immersed in many different points of view daily.

New York also has a broad community of all types of artists, whereas LA has a broad community of people trying to make movies and TV shows. Artists in other mediums are a curiosity in LA. There's more word of mouth about theatre, performances, and artistic expression in New York. In LA, theater isn't nearly as valued or supported, but there is plenty of it because plays are easier and cheaper to mount. So you can do more plays in LA, and there are very good dedicated theater groups who put on top notch productions. The downside is that professional people in LA don't see the benefit of plays. They have a habit of not attending even when they say they will, or sending an assistant to watch a play for them. Conversely, just getting into a play in New York is much harder, but can lead to a career, as theatre is taken very seriously. Good stage work in New York could get you an agent. Good stage work in LA could get you noticed by a casting director and might lead to a job that could get you an agent.

So you will be taken seriously in New York due to your training and time spent doing plays, but you face stiffer competition getting paying jobs because there are far fewer of them. Whereas, the fact that you played diverse roles in great plays on great stages with good people means very little in LA. It's more about what films and TV shows you have been in, and how good your tape is. The bulk of opportunities for high paying, career building jobs is clearly in LA.

The stereotypes of people's sensibilities in the two towns are that LA people are all phonies and New Yorkers are all angry. I have lived in both places and have met both types in each. It's a silly discussion, but one that a lot of folks *love* to engage in. Most New York actors never really go far outside the island of Manhattan, which is 23 square miles and houses 1.7 million people. Los Angeles is 465 square miles and houses 3.8 million people. Maybe that will give you an idea of why the pace quickens in New York as opposed to Los Angeles.

So, weather, affordability, ease of living—LA. Diversity, greater artistic access, on-foot travel—New York.

Now the safety factor can be argued for a long time, but I will go on record as saying (with no statistics consulted) that New York is the more dangerous place. New York gives you access to everything in the world, but everything also has access to you. You are simply in the crowd for more of your day.

LA feels safer because for so much of your day you're in a car, restaurant, or mall. You don't mingle with the population so much. I have friends from New York who say they feel safer there, but having lived in both places, I still feel that LA is a safer place to live.

Hype

SELL THE SIZZLE, NOT THE STEAK.

You cannot avoid the overwhelming hype-monster in America today.

You also cannot take any of it to heart. I find it dangerous to the actor's process in four ways:

1. Publicity is manufactured, written, and cultivated by the stars themselves. Those infamous Stars on the Walk of Fame in the sidewalk on Hollywood Blvd. aren't awarded by a committee that deems certain stars worthy. The stars themselves (or their "fan clubs") have to apply, meet the committee's approval, and then pay a $7,500 fee to get one. It's self promotion, but surely it never gets portrayed that way, does it? When did you ever see the unveiling of the star where the celebrity said, "Well my publicist said this would up my price as

an actor, so we worked like hell to convince the committee to pick me, and it was the best eight grand I ever spent"? Don't they all say, "I'm just so shocked that I would ever be here. It's a huge honor"?

There is a popular movement among actors to portray themselves as unwitting benefactors of the world's lust for their participation on screen. There are no reluctant stars, only ones who pretend to be. Clear your mind of the idea that any of these big names are there because the business just keeps forcing them to make movies, or that they really had no idea what was happening to them while their career was burgeoning.

The stars themselves construct the image being put out by magazines, including the rumor rags at the supermarket. The publicity machine works hard to make everyone believe that its client is just trying "to live a normal life despite all the well deserved riches and accolades that are being thrust upon them."

Don't believe it.

I say this because I feel it creates the unreal expectation in the newcomer that he needs to be a dedicated, growth-oriented artist, and at the same time, reluctant, free from struggle, and falsely modest about how it all happened. When you hear stories like this over and over, you can start believing that landing work is nothing more than a magical happening. As you continue to absorb the myth that your career should just happen for you, then you assume you aren't one of the chosen and that your honest efforts are wasted. Remember, hard work, desire, and training got you where you are. Keep that in mind, because the truth is that's how everyone got where they are. The way a publicist spins their client's actual struggle to manufacture sympathy or excitement in the marketplace is just that—spin. Don't ever let your honest approach to creating be corrupted by something as false as spin.

2. Hype lends itself to the perception that the journey to success is easy for everyone else. It will always appear as if everyone else gets the big easy breaks while you suffer away, straining your last functioning nerve to get through your day.

Don't believe it.

Overnight success doesn't exist. Right now some of you are saying, "What about so-and-so?" I will bet you the actor you read about who was "just DJ-ing at a party and got hired on the spot" had some desire to be an actor and had even taken classes. It's hard to convince a studio to rest their 20-to-100-million-dollar movie on the shoulders of someone who has no idea how to act, or any real desire to do so. Yes, there may be the once-a-generation-young-phenom discovery, but it is hardly a reliable career path. Life-sustaining acting work doesn't fall in the lap of the passing stranger who is free of ambition to be an actor. The odd TV episode or commercial may, but a career doesn't happen that way. The danger of reading and believing these untruths in the media is that you may start believing that if success is to come to you it *should* be effortless, like it was for so-and-so, who was just playing baseball in the park when the director saw him and cast him right then and there.

3. Hype may also start to dictate how you go about your work. When you read that a director says that the star of his movie "stalked me until I finally turned to him and said, 'You can play the stalker,'" it's easy to say to yourself, "I should do that!"

Don't believe it.

This is the stuff that makes great laundromat reading, but I promise you there's no director in Hollywood who will respond to stalking positively. If anything even remotely like that did happen, it was a harmless, spontaneous stunt that got blown out of proportion for the sake of the hype that helps sell the actor or film. If you start to forgo the work of acting to create a stunt that will get you noticed, you will lose focus and probably end up more embarrassed than successful.

Do not let the hype steer your process. Craft the growth of your artist from real data, not hype.

4. My last hype issue is about that "elusive, intangible quality" casting directors, directors, producers, and studio execs love to tout when fawning over some actor or actress. You've heard this said about every big star: "They have that *thing* that just can't be explained, that *star quality* that you have to be born with."

I find this idea dangerous for the young actor because in your search for the path to success you may try to emulate someone else's magic, or worse yet, strive to create an intangible.

I'm going to tell you what that magic is, and what that special spark is, and all the other words publicists have found to describe someone's star power.

Ready?

It is that the person is being himself or herself better than anyone else does. It is the actor being very good at allowing her authentic self to emerge, indulging her weaknesses and strengths. Genuineness is always interpreted as magic because so few people have the confidence to be really authentic in life, let alone on screen. Haven't you met a quirky person in your travels that by doing nothing more than being his quirky self has absolutely captivated you? Sure, some people are more interesting than others, but all of us are terribly interesting when we are at our most sincere.

Mind you, in my opinion, most of the time this is just a journalist trying to create excitement by using those words to describe someone whose performance wasn't really all that magical. Consider any major star and think about how many times you've read how their spark makes them a worthy superstar, and ask yourself how many times you have felt really touched by their work.

It's all hype.

The bottom line is that doing the hard work of being your best, honest artist is your "can't-put-into-words" magic. It's all you have to offer, so offer it with enthusiasm. And be on the lookout for hype.

Think about this story. A major studio executive told me that whenever the industry trade magazines reported on her company's projects, they always had the facts wrong in some way and always made the situation, deal, or project sound better than it actually was.

Now, even though she knew in her head that the trade papers lean toward building a simple story into a blockbuster, whenever she read good news about some other company's great success, she got jealous. Funny, huh? Even though she knows from personal experience that what she's reading has been hyped up, she still gets that knot of jealousy about the exciting heights that are supposedly being reached by others. It means we are all human and want to believe what we read word for word, especially when it's damned exciting.

As you learn more, you will be able to read a story and estimate the probability of its truth. Rarely do you get to read or watch a full, unedited interview, and when you do, as interesting as it may be, doesn't it lack that certain provocative quality of hype? Doesn't it become more about communicating than selling?

Be on the lookout in yourself for a tendency to believe in the hype to make your personal journey feel more exciting. We all write our glowing press releases in our heads and answer questions from imagined interviews. It's fun to dream about that level of importance. Be sure it's just fun, and not seen as the goal. You cannot deepen your work through hype. You can enjoy hype only as a consumer.

Rumor travels faster, but it don't stay put as long as truth.

—Will Rogers

Pictures, Resumes, and Demo Reels (Tape)

THERE REALLY IS NO SUCH thing as a personal appearance in an attempt to meet an agent or casting director. Knocking on doors doesn't get a meeting. Your picture and resume ("pic & rez" as they say) are always your entry point. They are dropped off, usually in a box by the front door, away from the staff, for later review. What the staff pulls out of that envelope (or what they see in an online submission) is all they can know about you. This is why your pic & rez are very important.

So they will be the point of much conversation and frustration. Take comfort in the fact that there are many good photographers who know exactly how to shoot a great headshot. This should be a fun project for you, because you get to control it. The photo shoot cost can be shocking, but know that there is always a way to get things done with good results for what you can afford. Yes, spending the money on a pro who has a stylist to make you over and who shoots six rolls can guarantee great results, but a friend who is competent with a camera can yield a good usable picture. Pictures are really over-worked and over-thought.

In picking a photo, understand that *everyone* has an opinion on what your picture should "say." Your friends, parents, acting classmates, casting associations, the doorman, the cabbie, and your doctor instantly become experts on headshots if you let them in on the debate. I will tell you this before you shoot: limit your sources when asking for help. Your agent (if you have one) will want you to use his choice above anyone else's. This can be touchy if you don't like his choice.

As you try to choose your headshot, consider that prospective agents and the casting world *hate* it when the actor or actress they call in looks nothing like his or her picture. Keep this thought in your mind as you choose your headshot. If you give out a headshot you have a responsibility to send that exact person in that headshot into the room when they're called.

Does that mean that any time you change your hair or appearance you need a new headshot? Yes. If you dye or cut your hair or noticeably change something in your everyday appearance that isn't temporary, get a new picture.

There is no value in having an artistically intense picture of yourself if it was a photo-shoot-only occurrence.

In case you just thought, "But don't I have to get in the door any way I can?" consider this new idea: "I need to get in the door, but, more importantly, I need to get back in the door after my first time through." If your picture gets you an appointment, you never want the casting person or agent to come to the waiting room looking for the person in your picture and then look disappointed when they see you. Misrepresenting yourself through your picture may sound like a good idea to get started, but why start out with a stunt? This is what a glamorously flattering, over the top picture is—a stunt. Why start your relationship by disappointing them? You have control over this element, so take it.

Pictures that flatter and accentuate one part of your body get put in files for the day they need an actor with that body part for hire. So, ladies, if you are big breasted and you make that the center of your picture, understand that your picture is saying, "I'm breasts, and I can say lines too." The same goes for tattoos, long hair, big muscles, cowboy hats, and sunglasses. You are reduced to that element alone.

Choose a photo that looks like you when you walk through the door, plus or minus 10 percent. It can be slightly flattering, but just slightly. As you look over your choices you will surely get bogged down with what each picture says about you. "In this one I look intense," and "This one says serious actor." Have fun looking through them, then take my advice and choose the one that says, "I know what I'm doing as an actor and this is my face," or "If you're looking for a good actor that looks like this, here I am." That simple? Yes. Keep in mind it is a picture, not your entire acting repertoire frozen into one frame. Don't ask your picture to relay that you're a zany, serious, classically trained, improv-savvy, edgy, yet intellectual artist. You will impress them with all that after you're in the room—the room you got in because they responded to how you really look. Your picture will hopefully garner calls, but you *really* want to be sure they are the right calls.

The second element to consider is that even if your agent, your friends, and your priest all agree on the best picture to use, it must be a picture *you* like. You have to feel good about pulling it out of your bag and handing it to someone. There's nothing worse than an actor squirming in his chair over comments, negative or positive, concerning his picture. It says you are not in control of your identity, and that it's up for grabs by anyone with an opinion of you.

If your agent, or someone else along the way, advises you to use a photo you don't like, remind yourself that it's your privilege to ruin your career by not taking their advice and following your own intuition. You'll find plenty of advice along the way, but ultimately you have to steer your own course. If anyone's going to ruin your career with bad choices, let it be you. Bad advice falls like rain, good advice sprinkles very lightly in small drops that you must carefully catch and use wisely.

Every agent has heard a million bashful comments from prospective clients concerning their hate for the camera and how uncomfortable pictures make them. Yawn. Save yourself from becoming a cliché by embracing your headshot so you can hand it out with no apologies and no explanations. Ladies especially have always had to downplay a flattering photo in false modesty. Don't pretend you don't know who you are because your beauty shows up in a picture. This goes for everyone. Own everything that shows up in your picture, or don't use it.

You will probably over-think your picture's mass reproduction. The use of digital technology has made the quality of reproductions improve to the point where you can trust that what is in your original will be on your duplicates. Just remember this: you won't be judged on the quality of the picture as much as on what's *in* the picture. Don't be too persnickety about the quality of the reproduction paper. Lithos and laser color copies are fine, and photos are certainly nicer, but they are never scrutinized by any casting office or talent agent on the basis of what they are printed on, or for that matter, if they are color or black and white. Most repro houses make you pay up front; don't sweat it. You can judge the quality of their work by the many photos on the walls that always adorn those places. If for some reason you don't like the outcome, they will usually entertain a rational conversation about it and redo them for the sake of quality. Places like these make their money on return customers. They want you happy.

You can also over-think the many format choices available in the setup and layout of your picture. Border, no border, type face choice, name on the front or not, landscape or portrait orientation, and so on. Just be sure you make choices that have you feeling smart and strong so that you can look everyone in the eye as you hand over what is effectively your business card.

The Resume

This is pretty easy. Don't give your height, weight, birthday, or sizes on it; that's for commercials only. Don't include your address, just a contact number. The layout should be basic and simple to read. If you spend too much time filling it up with senseless information because you're embarrassed about all the blank space on the page, that's what will come across. Remember that you're doing this for the first time, but the people reading it aren't.

The impulse may be to invent credits that will create the illusion of experience. You may think you'll gain instant credibility by having worked in *Rocky 5*. After all, how many people remember the cast of that movie? It's an uncomfortable day when you're in the room with the casting director for that movie and he catches you in your lie. If you worked hard to get into the room, why kill it with something as dumb as a lie?

What you should do is think hard about every role you've ever done anywhere and creatively express it in the best possible light. Consider every marketable skill you have and find a creative way to express that under the Special Skills heading. Don't be coy or cheesy with it, just think about it. There is always some skill we forget we have, or a role we forgot we did, that will make us proud the day someone in an audition says, "Really? You can do that?"

Put yourself in the best possible position by listing only those experiences you can discuss and follow through on. I have been asked about the places I did plays, the directors I've listed, and accents I've stated I can do. Most of the time the questions are about feeling you out, getting to know how you regard your work and your talent, not about whether you really are fluent in Croatian.

Your Tape

Your tape has become as essential as the picture and resume for attracting agents and casting people. You'll need to assemble whatever pieces you can to build a tape. You surely want film clips, not just video clips, and no home movies. You can get tape on yourself by doing student films. They always offer a copy as part of the payment for doing the film. Shorts done digitally are okay as long as they are done with an attempt at professionalism. A bunch of friends who get together with a simple video camera trying to get some tape out of it usually produce something that looks like just that and isn't as impressive as you think it is. There are also places that will tape you doing a scene in a professional production setting. I've seen taped scenes done in this fashion, and they're great, especially if you have no tape at all. There's no sense waiting for a job so you can get some tape—so you can get a job. Do what you can to get some footage of yourself.

Don't make any one clip too long. Leave the editing of your tape to a professional who builds these things all day. They work faster and they work with an editor's eye, not an actor's eye. Usually you bring them raw material, and they clip it. Then you talk about the order, and they do a nice job making it flow. Don't spend extra money on making it a cool presentation. *No montages*—casting hates montages! Don't make it slick with jagged cuts, music, or a creative front for the name credit. Simple is the best; get to the acting. No one was ever hired based on a great demo tape editing. This gives you a presentable tape for trying to get an agent, and after you have an agent, he has a tool to send out to acquaint the casting world with you. It costs money, but what doesn't? It's worth the money.

Many people have editing programs on their computers. With any amount of competence you should be able to cut something together that's fine. A pro will have the tricks to make editing not look like editing, but budgets are budgets. A clean picture of you in a scene where you get to show off your acting chops is all that is really ever going to be looked at.

Agents

An actor comes home to find his wife bound, naked, and in the closet. He frantically pulls the gag from her mouth and says, "Honey! What happened!?" Sobbing, she says, "It was horrible! Your agent came by to see you and when he found me here alone he forced himself on me and..."

The actor interrupts her abruptly, "Honey! Stop! Wait a minute!! You're saying my agent actually came to the HOUSE!?"

Getting an Agent

The good ones won't see you so easily, and you don't want to see the bad ones. It's a real tough spot. You have to feel your way through every call and meeting. Everyone has to start somewhere, and agents who work out of their homes or crappy offices shouldn't be judged solely by that. They may be working hard to get established too. If they've been working at it for ten years and they still have a crappy, yucky feeling office, bail out. There are plenty of respectable agents in the marketplace. Don't ever disregard your instincts about someone's creepiness because you feel like you have to start somewhere.

You also don't need an agent with a super flashy office. All you really want is someone enthusiastic about you—not just your type, gender, hair, breast size, sellable background—but you, your acting talent. That's asking a lot, almost too much these days. They will surely be looking at your physical elements as part of the package, but try to establish whether they are solely into your looks or they are interested in your skills too.

There will always be agents who will take you on to see if they can make quick money and dump you even quicker when they don't. Someone who sees you as a project worth working for is gold. Right now you are thinking, "I don't care as long as they get me auditions. I have nothing else right now." You could sign a contract with someone and find out he or she is a loser, and then try to end that alliance while you sign with another agent. If you then get a job with the new agent, you will be fighting off the first one, who's done nothing for you, but has a legal right to your money.

I had a friend who signed on with an "agent" who turned out to be a telemarketer by day and used his telemarketing job as his office. He never mentioned that when they met, but he had his agent rap down, and so she thought, "I'll start here." He did nothing for her, and when she found out what he really did during his day, she realized why. That was time she lost in starting her career. Why would someone take on clients and have agent meetings if he can't follow through, you ask? There are just as many agents and managers hoping for a break as there are actors hoping for *their* break.

Don't be discouraged when you hear, "Without credits I can't get you anywhere. Get some and come back." All that means is they don't want to work for you. Even when you have credits, you can just as easily hear, "Yes, you have some good credits, but they're not anything I can work with." It means the same thing. Just move on.

What you really want is to feel good about your agent. Try to find someone who will get on the phone and campaign with casting directors to get you in for auditions and general meetings. Initially, that's all an agent can do, so don't be put off by the small agency. Don't get married to the idea that going to one of the big established agencies is the only way to get started. A big agency might love you, take you on, and then bury you under their other four hundred clients anyway.

There is no sure fire formula to finding an agent you know will work hard for you. They will all sound a bit disingenuous and they all have a good "I love actors" rap down, so you'll have to go by how you feel around them. Listen for honesty in the agent's voice when he talks with you, and trust your gut. If you feel like he's being pretty square with you, then he's worth pursuing. Even if he turns you down at first, it's worth it if you have a good feeling about him to try back in a few months, reminding him that you met him and liked him and you now have these credits or are about to be in this show. You're building a relationship even when he's said no initially, because this business is a small circle of people, and you simply never know who you will bump into and how that next meeting can change your relationship.

How to Meet an Agent

The best scenario is to do a play, show, or film that makes you visible enough for someone to call and ask to meet you. But that's obvious, right? I mention it because you can easily overlook it and spend your time pounding the pavement or doing agent showcases, forgetting to do a real play or small student movie because you think you need to find a faster device for entry to their office instead of the traditional one. Be sure to keep your eyes on both options.

General mailings to agents can work, but from the data I've heard over the years, the odds are very low. It's an easy thing to try, with many companies offering mailing labels. At the very least you will gain knowledge of the many agencies and get familiar with their names and locations. There is always a possibility that you could get an agent this way, but I'd strongly advise you not to use this as your sole avenue. If a general mailing appeals to you, do it as an additional strategy.

Showcases and workshops are numerous in LA. They are run by people who charge actors a fee to appear in a night of scenes in front of invited agents and casting directors. This is a pretty good option. Ask who they invite and what their attendance percentage is. The casting folks receive a fee for watching these shows, so they usually attend. There are a lot of these places, so do a little research on the people they are inviting. Maybe you'll find that some showcase companies are better suited to you than others. Ones that invite casting directors for shows that you have a chance of doing would be a good place to put your time and money.

This controlled environment is the best way to showcase your talent. So consider creating a showcase night of your own with a group of actors that you bring together. It's just like producing a play—you rent the theater, rehearse, etc.—but the result will be infinitely better than doing someone else's buy-your-way-in showcase, both for you and the audience. A showcase night that you produce is an empowering experience.

How do you know whom to invite? There are many places to get agent or casting director mailing lists and labels. You can also place a notice in the Breakdown Services (a daily information service that every casting office subscribes to) on the CSA (Casting Society of America) website. Casting is used to being bombarded by showcase invitations, but it doesn't mean that they won't send someone from the office to see you. Be organized and do simple follow up calls to casting offices: "We sent you an invitation to our showcase and we're hoping to see you there!" It's a harmless call, so make it. You might hear a curt "yeah..." before they hang up, but don't be discouraged, it just means they're busy, not that you're not worth their time.

Another way to find an agent is to ask an actor friend at an agency for an introduction. You can also ask a producer or casting director to introduce you to an agent they like—that's really the best way. Ask your contacts to simply make a call for you to be seen by an agent. If during a meeting the agent says their agency is too big for you (which means he isn't interested in doing the work of getting you started), ask him to suggest a better starting place.

Agents know other agents and agencies because they move around a lot. Ask them what or who they think would be worth pursuing. They love to be seen as experts. If they make a suggestion, you should make a key move right then. Ask them this question, "Is making an introduction call to (the agent they just named) a favor I can ask of you?" It does a few things. If they do it, it gets you an appointment sooner with the agent they suggested. It also gives you practice in asking for what you need from an agent instead of always feeling like your job is to be passive. It makes you look like a savvy career person who's asking for help from another professional. These kinds of calls are commonplace in other businesses, but actors don't always know whether it's appropriate to ask, nor are we ever given the language to use. Give it a try if it comes up.

When You Get a Meeting with an Agent

Read this now, and remember to reread it before you go in to the actual meeting. Having tape is essential. Most agents will say, "Send your tape, and we'll have a look and call you if we like what we see." There may be a few that will still meet you and ask you to do monologues, but I haven't heard of that in a while. If you do get to do that, be sure they turn off the phones and lock the door for your three to five minutes. It's not too much to ask, and having someone walk in or call during your time will surely distract them, and you. And don't forget to turn off your own phone.

In the meeting do your best to enthusiastically interview them. The meeting will never show your acting talent. They are feeling out who they are potentially going to work with. "Does she have pop?" "Does he have bedroom eyes?" That's about all they can get from a meeting. Ask them about their lives, their careers, their favorite movies, their biggest triumphs, and what keeps them in this crazy business. It will flatter them and calm you. They are trying to determine how dedicated you are, how big a pain you might be, and if you're as sexy in person as your picture made you look. They want to know if you're going to flake out on them, if you're a prima donna, or if you're clearly hoping they'll make you a millionaire despite your insecurity or lack of talent. They'll probably also ask you what type of work you will and won't do, like commercials, soaps, or industrials. Be very honest about that. Don't go to an audition you're not interested in and then do bad work that sends negative feedback to your new agent.

The meeting may go well and end with the agent saying that they need a consensus among the other agents at the agency to sign you. At bigger agencies each agent has projects they are responsible for, so every agent will be representing you on the projects they cover. Getting a consensus is really just asking every agent if they think they can make money from you. It's also a buffer for that agent. They don't have to tell you they don't want to work with you—they can use the other faceless agents as a way of remaining friendly with you while still saying no. Or they might really fight for you, but still find that someone at the agency has a problem signing you. So, what do you do with that? Maybe two things.

First, you learn from it that rejection is a facet of the business and it's a function of the fact that agents are trying to balance self advancement and fulfilling their job descriptions while promoting the best interests of their clients. So they might not be judging your person, talent, or persona, because they might just not see you as the person who will further their career. No harm, no foul. It doesn't make them bad people. It makes them a bad match for you. This is good to know—move on.

If they don't want to sign you, but the reason is just trepidation, consider that there is such a thing as hip-pocketing, where they don't sign you, but they send you out on auditions and see what the feedback is—a no-promises trial period. If you do well, they sign you. Knowing this mechanism is in place in the industry, don't be afraid to say, "I really like you and your agency and I'd really like to be a part of that, so let's not let this stop us. I'm not afraid to let my acting talk for me, so would you consider hip-pocketing me for six months?" It's not pushy to ask. It's assertive. Also agent's and manager's assistants are often allowed to hip-pocket actors. That isn't a bad scenario if it gets you auditions. If you meet an agent's assistant standing in line at

Starbucks, don't be afraid to simply ask the question, "Are you allowed to hip-pocket clients?"

Signing with an Agent

We are in a holding pattern as of this writing in terms of a SAG contract with the agencies. Traditionally you were protected by the SAG TV and Film contract for agents. Not currently. It's the Wild West. Agencies now ask you to sign a GSA (General Services Agreement) and this will be clearly in their favor. Beware of wording like "10 percent in perpetuity," meaning for the rest of your life, whether or not they're still your agent. Any agency contract should be faxed to the SAG contract division; they'll review it and counsel you on it. A review of the contract will sometimes lead to a negotiation with the agent. Don't feel like you have no right to negotiate your first, second, or third contract with an agent. Until there are uniform protections through SAG you have to look out for yourself where your agency contract is concerned. You are a business, and so are they. Contracts are built to be two-way, not one-way. They will ask for the world, you will agree to what's fair.

If you are not in the union, do some research, find an entertainment lawyer, or look at what a SAG member has done with a similar GSA. Do this for sure! Contracts can come back to ruin your progress if you don't take care of them properly to begin with. Talk about becoming bitter—try paying an agent who didn't even get you the job, just because they have a contractual right to a commission. That'll make you bitter, so prevent it from happening.

Most agency contract questions can be directed to the SAG Agent Relations Department. They will walk you through the whole process.

Many additional contracts are included with the main GSA. Read them all. Agencies always attach a bank form or check authorization form to sign, which says you give the agency permission to cash your checks on your behalf. This means your paycheck gets sent to the agency, and they deposit it into their account, deduct their commission, and then send you a check for the rest. It has become standard business to sign this, but I don't think you should. I hate this process. I feel like I am the earner, so I do not sign that agreement. Instead, I take my paychecks, make a copy, and mail the agency a commission check. You should do this too. It protects you, but you must be diligent in your accounting and your timing.

I haven't been cheated, but agencies have sometimes taken their time in paying me or somehow sent my check to the wrong address. Paychecks have also been sent in error to old agencies who have "forgotten" to tell me they had them. So after a few years of the standard practice, I made the change, and I have always maintained this status. The production company doesn't care where they send a check, so it's not an inconvenience to them. I'm sure your new agent will pressure you with, "That's how we do it here," and you'll feel like it's rocking the boat to say, "I don't want to." Agents like to collect their monies first, keep their accounting straight, and eliminate the hassle of chasing down an actor for money. Not signing this authorization may be tough to do before you establish yourself as reliable, so just do what makes you comfortable. A lot of actors sign it because they don't want the hassle of doing their own accounting. Don't be that lazy!

About the Agents Themselves

There are very nice agents whom you will like personally and will want to include in your "family." A good agent will stand by you in the lean times because of the relationship you have with them. Sadly, they are the minority. Be careful, you can get your heart broken. Remember, it's a business and it will always be a business. In theory, agents work for you, but they don't see it that way, so don't bring it up. The reality is, in the beginning, you work for your agent until you become such a money maker that she includes you in the minute decisions that will make you feel like you're directing your career.

Your agent may withhold information from you that she gets about potential work because it doesn't mean real money to her. If you are on a TV show and get offered a play in Louisville, you may never hear about it. If you receive two offers, the one that is more lucrative will be lobbied for harder and the lesser will be demonized. Things that might make you a better artist, but that your agent doesn't stand to profit from, will never be explored. So don't think that your agent is the best judge of what to do for your career. They know a lot about how the biz works, but they also work the biz to suit themselves. They have as much of a right to look out for themselves as you do. I am generalizing, but I am doing so with a 98 percent accuracy rate. No agent will own up to this; they can't. They can't tell an artist that the artist will be nothing but commerce to them. Just know that when they say they are thinking of your career, they are also thinking of their own career.

Agents have enormous pressure on them to make their agency money. They get no credit for representing the person who has ten Outer Critics awards and five Back Stage awards. If it doesn't translate into money, it means nothing to the boss. Also know that it's a "personal relationship" you're ruining when you want to leave them, but it's "just business" when they dump you. This will be the syndrome for the rest of your career. Just be aware of it.

There are also very nice agents that work hard for, and honestly care about, you. Someone will have to work pretty hard to get your career started, and for that they agree to 10 percent. Your agent will be in the trenches with you, fighting to get you seen, and fighting to get you more money when the time comes. But don't ever lose sight of the fact that it's always business first. You will surely want to show your agent loyalty if your career advances, you start getting better jobs, and you are poised to be offered big roles in big projects with great directors. The news here is that there is a hierarchy of agents. A long-time veteran explained it to me this way: "If they (CAA, ICM, UTA) ask you to sign, you sign. They are the big leagues, and your career is fragile. The opportunity may never come again for whatever reason. So you go and you play in the big leagues. Your smaller agent knows the business, they'll recover." I offer that as advice only. Many people have done well by staying in a small place where they are a big fish. Real loyalty is hard to find, and if you think you have it, then it's worth keeping. I just say again, real loyalty is hard to find.

I had an agent dislike a decision I made while working on a big feature film. So while smiling at me, he quietly directed his agents not to push for me on big projects any longer. He didn't like how my decision reflected on him, and as such, he didn't put himself, or me, in that position again. My untenable situation on location overseas became cause for his embarrassment here, and he took it out on me. Why didn't he back me? Well, to my face he said he did, but ultimately it's a business, and he made a business decision. Unfortunately, it was a decision that wasn't in the best interest of me or my career. He did what he thought was best for the health of the agency. I was a client there seven more years before they phoned me one day to say they could no longer service my career. The fact that they had stopped submitting me on big projects was something I learned after I was gone.

I've had very good relationships with my agents as well, but only after I got clear in my head about the fact that we are partners in business.

Random Things About Agents

Here are some things you will always hear from agents: "It's really slow." "Pilot season looks very thin." "It's going to pick up soon." "You need new pictures—this one is too old/not any good of you." (Even if they chose it.) "You're out of pictures, order more," or "You're low on pictures, order more."

The instant you get a job, they want to be thanked for getting it for you.

The instant you don't get the job, they want to know what you did wrong.

They'll always tell you they hurt with your losses too, but remember they have a paycheck, while you don't.

One of the few daily perks they get—and a really fun thing that they look forward to—is when they get to give you the good news that you "got the job!" So take the time to share the exciting moment with them. They deliver more bad news than good, and even though they're practiced at being the messenger, it's a tough place to be, so don't take it out on them when the news is bad.

After they close a deal for you, they will all claim they got you more money than anyone else could. (Be sure you thank them for it!)

Don't expect them to be inspired or creative. You are the creative one, they follow the status quo. Don't let them dash your enthusiasm for any creative ideas you may have.

Agents change agencies about as much as actors do. They all complain about how the last place was hell, and enthuse about how the new place is a breath of fresh air.

They will offer acting advice. Things like "Make stronger choices," or "Go nail it," or "You have to blow them away." All really useless, obvious stuff, so just ignore it. They don't see it as insulting or condescending, but it may come across to you that way. It's never based on any real understanding of your craft. They're just trying to rally you, to engage you on that level. Just know that throwing around the jargon of your world is what they think goes with being a good agent, and hear the compliment in it that they are fighting for you, but don't, by any means, take it seriously. I say this because it can give you the idea that your agent knows what it takes to "blow someone away." He doesn't. But when we get to that scary place where we're sure everything we've tried hasn't worked, we might start trying other things, like the empty advice of our agent. Agents don't know what makes a good performance happen. They just know that you need one to get a job.

The funny thing about this is that they get really, really insulted if you offer advice on how they should do their job. So keep it in mind when you deal with them. If your conversation ever veers into how they could better do their job, you will most likely face strong, caustic resentment.

What Can I Do to Cultivate the Relationship?

Your first auditions are crucial. You will probably not get jobs at first; callbacks will probably be the first sign of success. Work to impress the casting person with your attitude and preparation. Make friends in the room. These early auditions are to meet people, have them see your work, and yes, try to get a job, but they mostly work to confirm to your new agent that you are worth his time and jobs are soon to come. So give your audition preparations the time they require. You are taking your agent's reputation in with you. He will judge you, and feel good about his decision to work with you, by your feedback from casting.

I had an audition early in my career that was a difficult, rage-filled, highly emotional, physical scene. I told myself that the challenge would be to really excel at that scene in what I knew to be a small room with no help from the casting director playing the other part in a fight. I went all out, and used what little the room offered as a set, but mostly I let fly with the real feeling I had for the scene. To this day, fifteen years later, when we talk that casting director mentions how great that audition was. The film was never made, but he called my agent to say he was blown away and I'd be called in for everything he had coming down the pike. At a time when I was new, this was pure gold. When there's no money being offered, great feedback is the next best thing for your agent to hear. Your prep and execution are crucial in the beginning.

Most agents like occasional drop ins; they're called "walk and waves." You stroll through the office, not totally interrupting them in their work day, but waving hello with a big smile and a thumbs up. Bring along a little food, a pastry, or candy. Who doesn't like a little gift in the middle of the day? I used to stop by and bring a whole steaming pizza to my New York agent because I knew the office was always hungry at about 4 pm. Wasn't I a hero on those days? Is it sucking up to them?

Of course. Agents live for that, so play it to your advantage. You are thinking now about your budgetary concerns, right? Get creative. There is always a way to flatter them with a little something that says "I brought you something, because I appreciate the work you do on my behalf."

Can I do that over the phone? Yes, but until they are well known to you, this is a feel-your-way-through thing. You want to be sure that they really have the time for you, and they're not placating you because they feel they have to coddle the needy actor or actress. If you feel like they do have a minute, make sure you have more than yourself, your career, or your insecurities to talk about. Talk about their kids, their hobbies, their weekend, or who they're dating. "I'm just checking in," will surely be met with "I'm on it! Not much happening" in the slow times, which becomes "Waiting to hear" in the busy times. So be sure you say, "I know you're busy, but I wanted to catch up with you. How was the weekend in the Hamptons?" They love gossip as much as anyone. Later in the conversation you can throw in casually, "Any news on the ____ project" or "What's the next few weeks look like?" Better yet, allow them to mention what's happening in your career. It's not as if the topic ever goes away between you—your agent knows it's what's always on your mind. Let them get to it their way, and remember what I said about telling them how to do their job.

Isn't this all a silly dance to make contact with my agent? Sure. You can get by with not having a lot of contact with your agent, but there is something to be gained by having an easy social relationship with them. It's practice for the future of your business life. Being exclusive about who you are social with in this business is a dangerous practice, as everyone changes jobs and everyone knows everyone. So it's a good idea to cultivate a nice rapport with your agent and thereby make every encounter with him less tense on the "Did I get the job?" score.

Is My Agent Working?

I see other actors my type auditioning for something and I haven't even heard of it. How am I supposed to handle this? This happens all the time. If you get wind of an audition that you think is right for you, how do you handle calling your agent to inquire? Delicately. They get this call a lot. Be sure you treat it like a simple inquiry, free of any accusation or paranoid tone in your voice (and that tone can creep in, trust me). Here is what you do: just put it out as information for them to please check on. You never say, "Why aren't I in on this?" I like to say, "I bumped into a guy I see at every audition you get me (notice the acknowledgment of their effort with "you get me" instead of "I go on"), and he told me he was going over to read for this thing. What do we know about that project?" It allows them to say, "Let me look into it" or "Yeah they're looking for people who can also speak Spanish for that."

This approach saves you from looking desperate and untrusting and it saves them from getting defensive. It's a tough place, because there is always some project that they will not know about off the top of their heads. By just tossing this information at their feet without judgment, you increase your odds of getting the desired return call, "Glad you said something, we missed it" or "We already submitted you for this, your appointment is tomorrow." (Even if they hustled to get the appointment after you told them about it.) You just want to put yourself in a position to get the audition; don't worry about why you had to bring it to their attention. Never try to nail down their failures in front of them. You can keep an account of missed opportunities for your own understanding of their proficiency, but don't bring it up with them. Agents are never going to be perfect and they will always, like anyone, take measures to keep themselves from looking stupid.

Remember Robert Altman's quote about Gosford Park? He said he could never make that film with American actors because even if he found a cast who wanted to do it, "their agents wouldn't let them." There's a lot of truth in that. You're saying right now, "I'll have control when I get huge," but I'm telling you it's a very political world.

When your career is in a slump, your agent will take no responsibility for it. When it's booming, it's because of their shrewd advice and deal making. When you don't make them money for a while, you have to know they are talking about cutting you loose. Nearly every actor I know has been cut loose from his agency at some point. After seven years with my agency, the owner—who took me to lunch when he wanted to sign me—had one of his *agents* call to say that they "couldn't service my career any longer."

What changed? The business hadn't, and I hadn't. I just wasn't earning as much, so they dumped me. While I was a series regular, they begged me to stay with them for life. A few years and no series later, they suddenly couldn't deal with the demands of my career.

Submitting Yourself

Actors can now submit themselves online for some projects. The real juicy film and TV jobs go out through services that casting directors and agents subscribe to. These services have rules about what auditions they put out for public consumption. Only legitimate agencies and managers can receive the choice audition notices. What some actors do is to find a way to get this information and then set themselves up as a phony agency so they can submit themselves for big films and TV shows.

This can get you some work, but it's only a way to get yourself enough work to entice an agent. You can't continue this forever. I do have one friend who has been doing it for years, but he is an established actor and submits himself using his real agent's contact info. He does it so he's sure nothing is missed.

The downside is that you might get caught in the lie. Casting knows which agencies they can trust to deliver talent. If you're not on their radar, they will regard your envelope with suspicion and check out the agency before they call you in. Like I said, you can probably get some work out of this approach, but you're better off just submitting yourself as yourself and not using the fake agency angle. If you get called in, it saves you from inventing answers about your agent. If the thought is that they won't open your envelope unless it has an agency name on it, I can tell you that casting opens everything. They decide on your viability after they have a look at your pic and rez. If you start the relationship with a lie, they have a right to throw your headshot away.

If you're lucky enough to get information about a good audition for yourself, work to get in without getting caught in an embarrassing situation.

Managers

MANAGERS CAN BE A GREAT entry point to representation. If a manager approaches you, it's worth a meeting, as he might help you get an agent and may have access that makes your start easier. Agents will talk about their access in the business, but managers have the ability to work angles and get things to happen in not-so-conventional ways.

But, anyone can get business cards printed up and call themselves a manager. Managers are not regulated by any franchise agreement. They do not need a license or have to put up the money to get bonded with the state to do business like agents do. That gives you less legal leverage, should you need it. SAG does not recognize them either. They are free to negotiate any commission they want for their services. It's usually 10-15 percent (in addition to the commission you have to pay your agent) but I have heard of higher. So you want to be sure to do the research on them and ask a lot of questions about their real ability and purpose. I have been in casting offices and have seen piles of unopened submissions in the trash and been told that they are from "fake" managers, so they don't even bother opening them anymore.

You should know that there is an unspoken undercurrent of contempt for managers from agents. Because agents are regulated and it costs more to become an agent, they are always seeking to expose managers as really being agents and making them conform to the same rules that agents do. You might think it's better to have two people looking out for you, and it is, but agents often see a manager as someone standing over their shoulder judging them. Not all agent-manager relationships are like that, but it is present.

What do managers do that agents don't? Nothing—they just have more tools to do it with. They can use any information they want to get you auditions. Agents have a protocol to follow, so they normally don't rock the boat with any casting directors, because they want to remain in the casting director's good graces for the sake of the many other actors they represent. Managers are known for, and are accepted as, royal pains in the ass. So they will rock the boat for their client. They don't represent as many people, so they have the time and focus to work for you. Talent agencies usually represent a few actors of the same type. How much fighting do you think they will do for you if they also have two or three other people they want seen for that role? It doesn't make good business sense for an agent to yell at the casting director about getting you in when they have three other people they are also going to campaign for. When your name gets dismissed, an agent moves on to his next best chance of getting the commission for that role. A manager usually has only one actor of your type and he will fight for you because you are his only concern for that role.

Managers are technically not allowed to negotiate your deals, but they all do. They cannot sign off on a deal—it has to be closed by an agent—but most of them get around that too if they need to. They are also not legally allowed to solicit you for work, but this is a gray area that the battle between agent duties and manager duties is waged on. They will do what they have to do to get their clients in.

Managers are much more sympathetic to your growth as an actor and they allow you more time to develop. They will stay by you in tough times and listen better to your concerns. Top managers are harder to get because they are usually small operations who want to stay small so they can service their clients. Good managers always have good working clients and a few big stars. They're good at schmoozing and are shameless networkers.

They are not one-stop shopping. Some claim to do everything for their clients, from publicity to public appearances, but they don't. They can't go out and hustle the corporate lecture circuit, for instance, but if an offer were to come to a client for something like that, a manager will spend more time sorting it out and arranging it than an agent would.

They very commonly will say, "We're not taking on any new clients right now," which is a polite "no." They are always polite in case they need to reestablish the relationship with you later. It's good policy.

They are also better strategists for your career choices. I have been backed by my manager in making choices for my family and in keeping my sanity over my bank account.

They are very helpful at finding ways for you to create your own opportunities and they will gladly roll up their sleeves to help you produce or write your own projects. They never mind looking for an angle to get you working.

Casting Directors

I auditioned for the lead character in a movie about my life. I didn't get the part. The casting director said I just wasn't right.

CASTING DIRECTORS CAN BE your best friends and your backstabbing enemies, but know this—they are *dying* for you to get the job. I call them the first line of defense.

And here is something you don't know: they need to impress the director and producer as much as you do. Yes, they have the paycheck for bringing you in and some have the long term job casting a hit TV show, but they also suffer the insecurity of not knowing when, or if, they will have another show to cast. It is a very competitive field, so they have to stay quite sharp about who is out there to solve their never-ending problem of "Who's gonna play this part?"

That's where you come in. Always be at your best. They will never put themselves in a position to be embarrassed, so if you do mediocre work or embarrass them with some bad behavior, you have strained their willingness to bring you in again. If producers don't like what they're seeing for actor choices they will hire a different casting director. A casting director friend told me the two things a casting director never wants to hear from their producer (their boss) after a casting session are "Keep looking" and "We have to talk." So a casting director's reputation is built by delivering a great cast, in a minimum of time, and in a seemingly effortless manner. They often don't have the time to coddle the genius hiding inside the tortured artist.

There are good, inspired, talented, and brave casting directors, but their numbers are a small percentage, and sadly, their opinion is often stifled by the egos above them.

There are many credible casting people who are nice and efficient, who find that they are hired for nothing more than to simply schedule and move people in and out of the audition room.

Bad casting directors take their toll on your career. You'll know them by the uncontrollable ego leveled at you, the little guy, because they can't risk offending anyone who will hire them. They are usually very vocal about your "obvious shortcomings." You'll know the difference between helpful advice and this type of senseless, ego-attacking drivel. Don't be scared of it. Instead, use it to sharpen your awareness of the fact that not everyone in a position of power knows what they are talking about.

How Do I Meet Them?

Showcases and those casting seminars where you pay to meet casting directors are probably the easiest way to meet one. General mailings don't work as well. Stopping in is usually a no-no, but they always have a drop box at their door. They are not unapproachable. They are usually just inundated with actors trying to meet them, so they have a system in place to meet new actors. Call the office and ask, "What is the best way to get a 'general' with the casting director?" The casting associate who answers the phone deals with this question all day and they will have some procedure in place.

You may have to jump through a few hoops or wait until "it's slow." You will have to be persistent and keep good notes on which office said what. Here is the rule for calling back. If they don't offer a specific date for a callback, use this sentence: "When would be a good time to call again and ask about this?" You give them the opportunity to say "a week" or "after March" and it gives you the beginning of your next call. "Hi, we spoke in December and you told me I should call back after March."

If you are simply being dismissed with no information on when you should call, then use this rule: one courteous call a week until they say "Please stop calling here." If you do that, you can usually get what you want without being a pest. Don't for a second think that it's your job to take the hint and go away. Make them say the words "You will never be seen here." Why? Because it's not good business to alienate anyone in showbiz, so usually they won't. That's your advantage *if* you stay courteous. Never let your frustration come out in your voice. Ask for the meeting every time like it's the first time you're asking—sweet and enthusiastic. Courteous persistence is a virtue, and no one will hate you for it. Annoying, entitled persistence is a nuisance, and they will dismiss you as fast as they can.

General Meeting

You will most likely start by having "generals" with casting directors. This is a sit-down chat where they just meet you and get a feel for your looks, your age, and your personality. Before you go in, do some research and see what movies, shows, or plays they've cast, and with which directors, so you can sprinkle the meeting with flattering questions about how they found that amazing little kid or how great they must be to have Spielberg use them exclusively. I'm surely not suggesting that you overtly ass-kiss. Just have some knowledge of their work so you don't spend the whole time talking about yours. These interviews can be very dry and pretty boring. They'll want to discuss your training, your background, your agent, your hometown, movies, stars, LA vs. New York, and anything they think will spark you to be your natural self.

This is a good time to make a friend. "Where did you grow up?" you can ask them right back. Be interested—you are getting clues as to how they like to be regarded and treated. Those are good mental notes for when you want to get back in their door. Ask them outright, "What, in your opinion, are an actor's worst habits?" They'll love that you're calling them an expert and that you're trying to start out on the right foot.

Don't get fixated on being edgy or clever or hot, thinking they will suddenly call all over town telling all their friends about the amazing new talent who just walked in the room. They are well practiced in the general meeting antics of actors. They're meeting you, not the "you" you hope they'll see and promote.

Your natural manner and passion for the subjects at hand will let them know whether or not you are ready, talented, professional, and fun to be with. Yes, you want to be honest, but always lean toward the positive. Negative remarks about fellow actors or movies come across as insecurity. Passion is one thing; attacks are another. It's okay to be honest about a movie you didn't like, but don't go off on some actor's performance thinking it'll make you look like you have more talent. It makes you look jealous. They also may have a personal relationship with the person you're talking about and may have high regard for that person's talent. Your damning remarks about them will make you look less talented. It's also their job to try to build a good team on the set. Since they know their director or producer's personal peeves and tolerances they're also trying to match personalities. They could love your talent but not think you and the director would get along.

Read Copy with Me

At some point they'll have you read a scene with them. They are generally horrible readers and not much will come out of the scene in terms of real acting. It's hard to get anything good to come out of you when the person across from you is judging your every choice during the scene, but that's how they do it. Know, going in, that they may drop some text on you and ask you to read right then and there with the age-old disclaimer, "I just want to get a sense of you, don't worry, it's no big deal." And it isn't, so do the best you can without apologizing. Just go ahead and read it. They're not really judging you for much more than appearance and the feeling that you know what you are doing. Your approach will tell them that. They won't really expect you to nail the scene or be a deep meaningful character.

If you know your process and you need more than two minutes to prepare, be honest and say, "I'm a horrible cold reader. I'd love the opportunity to go over this and come back tomorrow." This is when you might hear the second oldest disclaimer, "Well, in this business you have to be able to do things on the fly." Which is bull. I say this because I've always been given the material before I've gone into an audition. Improv auditions are the only auditions I've ever heard of where they don't give you any material in advance. All they are saying is that they don't have time to meet you again and they want to know you, which is good news. If you simply cannot pull it together and just do an easy, simple reading, tell them you're dyslexic and you can't cold read, but that you'll be happy to come back whenever they have time.

By the way, many well known working actors are dyslexic. It won't shock anyone. I sat through a table read of a sitcom once with a girl who is now a mega, mega star, who read so poorly that it looked like she would have to be replaced. Only after the table read did she admit to me privately that she was dyslexic. The next day in rehearsal, after she had the night to go over it, the producers watched in awe, and talked about nothing but her star quality.

At an Audition

Auditions *always* run late. Be prepared for it and use the time wisely. Don't get into the habit of thinking that because they always run late you can be late. Casting folks keep mental notes about who is and who isn't reliable. Be on time. They notice and appreciate it. Remember, they will not risk being embarrassed, and the one time they are on schedule you don't want to lose them as an ally because your lateness left them with an annoyed director or producer sitting in an empty room. They also talk with their peers. So there's a good chance your habits will precede you.

At the audition you may feel the impulse to connect with the casting director on a personal level, trying to bolster your relationship with them while they are in front of you. It's okay to say something brief on the way into the room or in the waiting room, but on casting days, casting directors usually don't have the time for small talk. Definitely don't do it in an audition. You can surely work within their time frame and send good vibes their way without ever sitting down in the audition and gushing over them. Be creative. What you do, if it is earnest, may come as a nice break to their long, repetitive day. So if you feel the impulse, remember to connect with them—don't make them have to connect with you. Let me stress this part again: when you compliment a casting person, make sure it's sincere. They are worn out by the perfunctory kudos. If you can smell a phony what makes you think they can't? It's insulting when an actor lobs a lame compliment over to them. So either say something sincere or say nothing.

On the walk in to the audition room there is generally time for quick dialogue. Go beyond the same old, "It's good to see you." I always say, "Thanks for thinking of me. You always take such good care of me and it doesn't go unnoticed." They never hear that. Actors almost exclusively talk about themselves and what the casting person can do for them.

In the room, before you audition, be sure you engage the right person with the scene by asking, "Who am I reading with?" Here is another place to reward the casting person. Right after the reader says, "You're reading with me," smile and say a warm, "Oh great!" This will also be a nice pat on the back to them in front of their peers.

When Finished

Do the casting director a favor—thank the people in the room gracefully and leave. You don't have to rush out, but help them by being considerate of their time issue. Spending more time in the room does not increase your chances of getting that job. In fact, staying longer could be doing the opposite.

If the casting director or their assistant trails you out of the room to get the next person, use that as an opportunity to quickly but warmly thank them. After all, their memory of you is what gets you an invitation to audition. Yes, your agent (if you have one) can jog their memory too, but they still have the power to exclude you. I'm not talking about shamelessly kissing ass (although they do love that). I'm talking about respectfully acknowledging their part of the process, as one professional to another.

How Do I Combat Getting Typed?

You don't. You accept it. Do casting directors type you? Sure. But you type yourself as well. You do so with your work, and I mean your *real* work, not the "I'm an actor, I can play anything" ego stuff all actors like to believe. No you can't. No one can. What you can play is up to those watching you. Accept that you are a type with the same acceptance you have for your own habit of judging everyone you see. Don't fight it. At first you will fall into a category by virtue of the things you can't change—your height, hair, eyes, skin, and ethnicity. We are what we are. These attributes have a way of being elastic if your work is something they love.

In the beginning you will have the opportunity to go in for a good variety of things because you are new, so do your work and let the typing discussion be theirs, not yours. You can get on the phone and convince people about what you can do, but in the room their opinion forms by what they see. Let your work speak for itself. The only way you can know that you have been properly typed is to do your best work all the time.

I'm sure you have that fear of being wrongly typed because some part of your persona is constantly misunderstood. That befalls many of us. Maybe you think you have to go into the meeting dressed a certain way or acting a certain way to counter some quality you've heard people tell you takes away from the real you. Let go of that. You cannot control what you are in the eyes of others, and even if you were able to mask something in a meeting, it will come out soon enough if you get the job. Just go in with the idea that you're going to give them a chance to meet the real you and let the impressions fall where they may.

Feedback

I have a saying, "Take the strokes, ignore the folks."

Feedback is so generic most of the time that you have to ignore 95 percent of it. I say this because usually by the time any feedback gets to you it's so bastardized that it is usually more harmful than helpful. Ignore it.

Now that's pretty dismissive, but as a rule, the process of getting feedback is so convoluted that the original intention is lost. Also in my experience, sadly, most of the time the intention isn't to help you in the first place. This is an odd, dysfunctional business of egos. Rarely have I found purity of intention and the sharing of good advice for one's honest personal growth. Usually the real message is, "If you hope to please me next time, you should..." not, "For the betterment of your artistic growth you may consider..." Why would I ever think anyone should have such a lofty goal as my growth in mind when giving feedback? Because that is the way it is usually phrased. But the feedback rarely speaks to your artistic self. It's almost always about your business self getting another lesson in how to deal with the many personalities that you will encounter on the road to getting a job.

For the sake of giving feedback casting directors dig around for some kind of answer. Even though your audition may not have been strikingly bad or good, they will have some kind of general feedback. Your agent calls them with questions like "Why didn't she get the part?" or "What did the director think of my client?" A casting director knows it's incumbent on them to say more than "I don't really know...it went okay." It makes them sound unprofessional, but it may well be the truth. They don't always know what the director or producers are thinking. So they give their impressions, and if they don't really have any strong ones, some casting directors have a propensity to say something anyway. Some harmless thing to have an answer that can easily be misinterpreted by the telephone chain of command and leave you feeling crappy about your abilities.

Your artist makes the distinction between useful and harmful feedback instinctually. Listen for it. Your talent is not at stake. Your business savvy is. Once in a while you will get a comment about your work that rings true. You know that feeling you get when a suggestion penetrates and rings the bell of understanding for you. That's when you say thanks and take it in. But when you are new to this process, the feedback can be all you live on in terms of approval, and you can easily fall into the trap of using feedback to inform your artist. It's dangerous territory. Casting people are not actors. They surely don't know how to get your best work out of you. So ignore most of what you hear and trust your common artistic sense to tell you what feedback is useful and what feedback is just someone else's ego spilling over on you.

Recently when a friend of mine asked for feedback on why he didn't get the job he thought he'd auditioned well for, the casting office came back with, "We needed to see ten emotions at once, and you only had five."

Can you see how something like that might cause one to think he is lost, or in the wrong place? That kind of feedback is destructive to a creative person looking to better their artist. Why? It's impossible! It's crap! It's obviously from a very uneducated casting person who overheard that somewhere and liked how it made them sound. No artist in the world would ever tell an actress she has to play ten things at once. It's not humanly possible. If you play something well and someone in the audience decides he saw ten things happening at once, that's out of your control. It's an opinion. It's not *ever* for an actor to think about. This is an incredibly stupid comment to make to a young actor because it opens the door to the idea that there is someone who can knowingly act ten things at once, on command, in an audition, but that you just aren't good enough to do that. A comment like this clearly comes from someone wanting to sound like an expert who's raising the bar for his little world of actors. It's damaging, stupid, impossible, and sadly, very prevalent in the acting profession.

Some time went by and I jokingly asked that actor friend about how he was dealing with showing only ten emotions at once. He said, "Oh, I fixed that. Now I give them twenty emotions at once and let them pull me back." I'd say he's dealing with that kind of feedback the best way you can.

Remember, They Are on Your Side

Casting people are very sympathetic to your process. They need you to be at your best, but they really don't know what the actor needs to get better or how that process works. They say they do, but they see only from the outside. They don't delve into the inner work, so don't take to heart what they might say about process. They will occasionally offer acting advice. It means they're cheering for you. Enjoy the compliment, but don't get too wound up in it. Remember, you are still the artist and you will do your part in cheering for them by always bringing your best attitude to their audition. That means you will take in stride whatever difficult circumstances they have: odd location, cold office, inconvenient parking, and a long, long wait. Never blame them. Never shame them. Always look for the light side of the situation and share their hardships with them. "I can't believe how comfortable you made me in a room with no heat. Thanks!" Or better yet, be the one actor who says nothing at all about it and delivers a great reading.

What Else Do They Do?

I don't want you to think that casting people have no influence in the casting sessions with producers and directors. They do. If the casting director is a big fan, he can be the very thing that's keeping you in the running. They also answer questions the producer or director has about you on a personal level. "Have you ever seen her be comedic?" "What's the buzz on this guy?" They will assemble tape on you (in addition to what your agent sends) for a director who is on the fence. They have strong opinions and love to add them to a creative conversation about actors. So be clear that they don't get final say or maybe even a vote, but they can influence the voters.

Their job also doesn't stop with finding actors. Their office is often the liaison for headaches in dealing with a newly cast group of actors and actresses. Even after the director's decisions have been made, casting directors still have elements they are responsible for, like negotiations and logistics. They have a big part in episodic salary negotiation and a hand in the negotiations for series regulars. In feature films they will also take part in negotiations because sometimes the business affairs people (the studio's negotiators) don't know who's who or what's at stake for the director. They know the budget for each project and how it's being diced up for the cast. Wouldn't it be nice to have them in your corner while the pie is being sliced? All of this suggests the idea that you want a friend speaking your name during the casting process and after you've gotten the part.

The Forgotten Ally

After a casting director gets you a job they love to hear how it went, what you loved about it, and another "thanks." Marion Dougherty, the grand dame of casting, said in a radio interview that Robert De Niro was the only actor who ever called her to thank her and just chat with her after she cast him. She said that actors generally forget about you until they need you again. I call casting director friends after seeing a movie they cast that I honestly thought was well done, and applaud them for the great cast they put together. They love to hear they are doing a good job. Who doesn't?

Most of the time when you call they can't talk to you, so leave a message: "No big deal, I just wanted to say hi." This is touchy when you're starting out, as it will be seen as ass kissing or pestering. Just use your good sense and choose your words wisely. "It was fun to meet you and talk about (insert parts of the conversation that will remind them who you are and what a fun time you had together!)." The follow up call is standard, but how you do it is what you bring to the table. To be yourself and say what you really feel is a nice way to relate to them. "I hope you'll come to my show, as I value your opinion," is nice. They've heard it all, so try to make it as real as you can. Your sincerity will most likely be the very thing that gets you remembered.

Some Fun Things

Things casting people have confided to me:

The director on a big budget film gave the casting director photos daily that were torn from magazine ads with the edict, "Find them. I like their faces. Bring them in, I want to read them."

After not getting a lead part in a movie I was told, "We literally flipped a coin because no one could decide between you and the other guy."

And one of my favorites was when I was told, "When you get to a TV network test (the big audition in front of the network execs), your acting really doesn't matter. They're looking at faces."

Now on to auditions themselves.

Auditioning

How many actors does it take to change a light bulb?

One hundred. One to do it, and 99 to say; "Oh, I could have done THAT!*"*

THE KEY TO AUDITIONING IS keeping your sanity through the process. The money will come and the jobs will come and the success will come *if* you're mentally prepared. I will tell you the things you can actually control in auditioning. Everything else is pretty well out of your control. As much as you want to think otherwise, there are only three things you can do in an audition to help the outcome.

I said before that auditioning isn't about finding the best actor for the job. Let me explain that statement.

If auditioning was about getting the best actor for the job, there would be an environment where actors could do their best work. As it is, it's an environment set up to see who can be a good auditioner. Only in the theater do they understand it's an interactive art—that a scene with two people in it will be realized only by having both people in it actually acting. They work from the perspective that if you want to see one actor in particular, you should put him in a place where he is the only one acting. So what do they gain by watching someone act alone? The knowledge that this actress can find a way to act in a one-sided, empty, vacuous situation. Their logic is that if you can do that, acting with another actor is only all that much easier. Flawed thinking at best, but it's the system in place.

Good auditioners are not necessarily good actors. Auditions don't necessarily reveal talent. Many very talented actors will say they are awful at auditions and hate the process. Auditions are built for the person who has the ability to be "really great" and "really exciting" for two minutes but may have no idea how to make sense of a whole character from the first act to the third, or how to make contact with another actor. "Nail the scene and you've got the part," is what's really going on here. You can count on one hand the producers or directors who can tell from your audition if you have any real acting chops. Most decision makers feel safe in the attitude, "If an actor doesn't have it here today, how can I trust he'll ever have it?" That's why the audition process is imperfect. If you ask me, it's highly flawed.

It's as if no one has ever heard of rehearsal or learning something from doing it more than once.

The problem is time. Casting moves very quickly. Beyond big budget feature films, very few projects have the luxury of time. Callbacks are usually quick and more about thinning the herd than seeing your work get deeper. Many times after you leave an audition, parts of the scene will become clear to you, but if you're not on the list for a callback, you'll never get the chance to show them that. They don't care about anything but the two minutes they've granted you. If you shine, you're in. If you don't, you're out. Time is money. Decisions make reputations.

So what are they looking for, if not the best actor?

Casting decisions are usually made by committee. So, the least common denominator usually gets the job. The actor who offended no one, potentially impressed no one, but was someone everyone could live with. This doesn't apply to the few directors who have real autonomy, but it's more the rule than the exception. They are looking for the best person for the job, not the best actor. The person whom everyone can live with and who will do a good job for the whole of the project, not just for the role, is what they are seeking in their casting. You, as an actor, get to concentrate on doing a single piece of the puzzle. Your focus is easy. Theirs is vast.

You think I'm wrong? Turn on your TV and ask yourself how many actors impress you. Have you ever wondered how they got on that show? That's how. They were the easy middle of the road choice. They definitely had something to offer the role—I'm not saying the janitor could wander in and get a job. I'm saying in many cases getting the job is more the result of surviving the inner office politics than a true measure of who was the greatest acting talent.

I'm also not saying that everyone who gets a job is mediocre. Talented people will always find work. Great, talented actors and actresses surely had to audition in their careers. They made it through, and their talent was uncovered. I'm addressing how the audition process can cause the talented actor to feel untalented by not getting the job. Being a likeable, easy, sharp, solid choice usually wins out. My point is that great acting isn't all you will be judged by. In not getting the job, you should not necessarily question your talent. You should look to understand the system better.

Putting Yourself in Charge

The system makes you the director, the writer, the actor, and the producer, all in one. It makes you find your opening night performance and deliver it into the room. You are free to create whatever you want with your two minute audition. So do that. Approach your audition like it's your turn to hold everyone in the room hostage with your work, instead of their holding you hostage with their decision. Have fun, and risk sharing yourself with them, because while directors and producers generally don't know how to tell you what they want, they always know what they want right after they see someone do it.

So I Have an Audition. Why Am I Shaking?

This is a very normal reaction, so how does an actor deal with the nervousness and fear of the process? First reread the previous paragraphs and see if understanding the process really does free you up to do your best work. The pressure is zero, because most of it is out of your control.

I have found that fear of the reading is one of three things.

1. *Too much focus on the big picture.*

You're thinking about what the world will become if you get the part, it becomes a hit project, and you become a household name. It's the ambitious mind at work. It makes the whole process exciting. It also has a way of burdening the acting process with results. Your mind is off the execution of the scene and it's on things like:

"My high school reunion will be *very* different if I get this."

"I'll see myself on billboards—oh my god!"

"If I get this, I'll be on easy street."

"I need the money so badly."

"It's *my* goddamn turn!"

There's an easy fix. Have fun for a minute with the exciting "maybes" this could create, and then refocus on the words, ideas, and intentions of the scene. Get prepared to act the scene like it was another day in class.

2. *The "they" factor.*

You fear that "they" (the people in the room) will find out you're an impostor. With this thought you're giving the producer's and director's opinions too much importance. You are congesting your creative mind with a need for their approval. Your fear of not winning their approval stops your creative mind from doing the scene well and winning their approval. You will go through thoughts like:

"I hope they like me."

"I'm gonna prove they were wrong not to hire me last time."

"They are going to applaud when I'm done."

As I said before, most of the time they don't know what they want and they certainly don't know more about you than you do. So don't sell short the time you spent learning about and cultivating your artist by going in and asking for permission to be you. You can nip this fear in the bud if you make the choice to see them as fellow artists—artists who respond to good work and take their best guess about what will work in their project, and nothing more. They are not the holders of your future. They are a part of your day today. They are not in charge of your fate, or your talent.

3. *You are not prepared.*

This is the most common reason for fear before an audition and thankfully the easiest to cure. When you are tense before an audition it's usually your mind informing you that you haven't done enough work yet, so take the time to find the spark that makes the scene clear to you and give them a real dose of what you see in this character. Suddenly, your fear of the audition will become impatience to get in there and act.

Good Habits to Have as an Actor

1. Clear focus. Ask yourself before you leave the house, what is my job today? Your job in an audition is to be prepared and do your best acting work. That's all. There is no way that you will ever get a job by going in to claim the job. You will get that job only if you go in to really tell your cheating wife you caught her and how bad it hurts—or whatever the scene is about. You have to act to get the job. "Go in and *take* that job!" is the positive-thinking-empowerment pep talk that some people try to sell as audition technique. That may help the insecure actor feel more positive walking in, but even with that attitude he will still have to act the scene out. Knowing your job and being clear about it alleviates the tension of thinking you have to be more than what you are, that you have to learn a way to market yourself in lieu of actually acting in the room.

It's like saying, "I'm determined to get married by next week!" and going to the church seven days later and hoping a partner, priest, flowers, and friends all just show up. You cannot go in there to get paid or to impress people. "*Take* the job," "Own the room," or any of those other phrases audition coaches tell you to do will not make up for mediocre work. These are just tricks you play on your mind to relax into doing good work. They are not things you can actively do to get the part. They just serve as a distraction from the fear of auditioning.

Should you be charming? Yes. Should you be warm? Yes. Interesting? Yes. These qualities all help, absolutely, but in doing those things, don't lose sight of your job, which is to act and to create a complete character. Have no expectations about the result. The result is not your job.

Your personality will certainly be an element in getting any part, but it will surely be the experience of your work that earns you a role, not how powerfully you came in and sat down. I don't know that I've ever heard, "His reading flat out sucked, but he sat down with such confidence that we're going to use him because of the way he took the room!" It doesn't happen that way.

Actors also fall into the trap of entering the audition with what I call their heightened personality. It's a bigger, usually false, forced charisma that's aimed at getting the people in the room to instantly like us, or find us really interesting or funny. We push because we feel that our time in the room is as well spent impressing them with our personality as it is with impressing them with our acting talent. I really don't think you can steer people to see you the way you want them to. You have to accept that every part of your behavior will be scrutinized and interpreted by different people differently. The difference between feigning interest and really being interested in what the director is saying is visible to those watching.

Confidence, and I mean confidence, not arrogance, shows up clearly in an audition. You'd be shocked to hear how often simple confidence is grandly rewarded with praise like "intense," "star quality," "edgy but vulnerable." The casting world loves to gush over someone who is the real deal—their real talented self.

2. Adopt this philosophy: "Getting there is the work." Make everything you do surrounding an audition (and the biz) that is anything but acting, "the work." Treat getting there as the work. Treat the waiting as the work. The terrible traffic, the crowded subway, the overflow parking is the work.

Then, put in your head that any acting you do (in the audition and on the set when you get the job), you do for free. This way, the instant you arrive to an audition (or the set) the work is over, and when work is over, what do we do? We relax. The grind work is out of the way. The hard part is over. The free, easy part, the part you know how to do, the fun part, is all that's left. Go over your pages. Reinforce your knowledge of the lines, and go have a ball with your audience. If you say you love to act, well, aren't you looking at an opportunity to walk in a room and do what you love? Act for free and it will lose the burden we connect with the term *work*. Adopt a new philosophy: "I act for free. When they pay me they are paying for all my time spent trying to get a cab or a parking space!" Audition from a place of fun, not work.

3. Adopt a "no accumulation" policy in your head. Every audition has to be treated as a separate entity. You cannot allow the rejection or instant feedback or weird occurrence that happened in other auditions to color how you approach the next one. I am speaking in broad terms here. Learn from every audition for sure, but for example you cannot assume that you didn't get the job yesterday because the producer hated your shirt, so you should never wear that shirt again. Or maybe he asked you a question and you could feel your answer turn him off for some unknown reason. You cannot allow superstitions to become rules of your auditions.

During one audition I was asked, "Who is your favorite baseball team?" and my answer instantly turned the producer sour. He clearly let me know that the only right answer to that question is "the Yankees." It's an odd thing to stand in a room with adults and have your audition come to a screeching halt before you even read for having the wrong baseball team allegiance. So, if that ever came up again wouldn't I have learned to answer, "the Yankees"? No, they are not my favorite team. Is it really that touchy in the audition room? That day it was, and I don't know why. I do know that I'm not going to try to guess at the right answer. I'm going to be me. My team is my team. I do not allow that room's weirdness to change who I am. In my paranoia to always do the right thing and get the job I could easily tell myself, "Lesson learned. Baseball is upsetting to producers, so steer clear." But I serve the process only by bringing who I am forward and letting the chips fall where they may.

Props and Wardrobe

My rule of thumb is to never bring in anything that isn't essential to doing the scene better. You can mime a phone if you have to do a phone call, or use your cell phone, but if you bring in props to help you look the part, they will distract from the reading. If they are integral to doing the scene, by all means bring them in, but with props, less is more.

With wardrobe, you do have to approach the audition as if those in the room have no imagination. So if it's a lawyer, wear a suit. If it's not that straightforward a character, then you should wear anything that helps you feel the scene better. But if you're wearing a silly hat to show you're zany, they will remember the hat and not you. Only bring and wear what really helps you realize the character.

And on the subject of wardrobe, this note is mostly for the ladies, but everyone should think about it. When dressing for your auditions, dress appropriately. The casting world is made up of more women than men. So, ladies, when you dress for sex in a scene that has no sex in it, it's noticed and criticized. This complaint has been expressed to me more than once. I'm sure you're thinking "But producers are men and they hire sexy!" Sure we've heard those stories, but I can tell you no producer is going to risk his show's success on a bad actress just because she had a great body and wore a revealing outfit. Same for you gents. If the scene doesn't call for ripped abs, don't walk in showing them.

In the Waiting Room

Never carry the hassle of your day in with you. If you feel uneasy while you're waiting and your mind is locked on a few if-only thoughts like "How am I supposed to do good work with the day I'm having?" or "If only I had gotten the sides last night instead of this morning, maybe I'd have a shot at this." Aren't these the same kinds of hurdles you faced in acting class or at school? Remember thoughts like "This play would be easy if I was the lead" or "My scene partner is driving me crazy!"? Same feeling. Same hassle.

Why would we let the crap of the day kill our inspiration? Getting through the struggle of your own mind long enough to pull together a nice reading can be the biggest part of an audition. So why would an actor create this obstacle for himself?

Fear—it's just your mind trying to distract you from the anguish of possibly doing bad work and disappointing the capable, wanting, artist within. Our insecurity about our work has us looking for a distraction or an excuse.

Sign in, sit down, and go back in your mind to good habit #1. "What is my job today? To go in and act this scene out with my best understanding of it. Focus, go through the pages for real, without distractions, and allow your artist to spin the beats of the scene over and over in your head, looking for some new meaning or possibility. You are creating fearlessness by sticking to the parts of the process you can control. Have fun, and *never* cower under the false truth that there is a way to get the audition dead right.

Bad Habits to Avoid in the Waiting Room

1. The waiting room is notorious for knocking you off your game. It's usually a stark, bland space with chairs or couches right next to the desk of the casting assistant, who is always on the phone talking about other actors. There will be plenty of opportunities to let fear kill your spirit. Everyone will look better for the part than you. You will often be sitting with a recognizable actor. Your fear might say you don't belong with real actors. The only reason you wouldn't belong there is if you didn't do your homework and you're not prepared. Keep this in mind: They remember bad work just as much as they remember good work, so don't go in and wing it. Do your best work, and don't let any of the waiting room games be anything but entertaining.

2. Many bad actors use the psyche out game. They talk a little too loud about how great their career is going. They rehearse too loudly. You will also probably encounter the moron who comes out of the room and says smugly, "You can all go home. They said it's mine!"

Or an actor who auditions early on will get a general overall note from the casting director about the scene in the audition but conveniently forget to pass it on to the other actors when they arrive.

Often you are given several scenes to learn, but at the audition a few waiting actors are told that the director wants to see just one of the scenes. This too doesn't get passed on to the actors who arrive after the announcement. I've been in auditions where an actor exiting the audition room wouldn't divulge which of the three scenes he just read so as to gain some edge or level the playing field in his eyes. It's stupid. Don't do it.

It's the mark of a real amateur, a real classless actor. It's also the mark of fear. I'm all for being fearless at an audition, but don't confuse the warrior mentality with attacking your fellow actors. I know a theatre director who sends the stage manager into the waiting room to hang out so he can bring back a report on which, if any, actors were being professional and which were being problematic. It's his feeling that a problematic actress in the waiting room will be a problem to the unity of the group, and moreover, to him, the director. Needless to say, anyone with a bad report from the stage manager isn't hired.

Treat your fellow actors with respect. They are not your competition. The producer's idea, the network's directive, the director's bad lunch is your competition. You and your talent are your own competition. Your fellow actors and actresses are the people who will become your friends, allies, and your biggest comfort when you need someone to understand your plight. This is an understanding you should apply to every aspect of your career. Be good, courteous, and helpful to your fellow actors. Not everyone acting alongside you today will continue acting. Many actors leave acting, but not the business. They become directors, writers, casting directors, and development and studio execs. I'm not talking about being friendly with everyone in case you need to suck up to them later. I'm talking about treating actors like friends and not competitors. You will be building a support network with your peers, and on the day when you are surprised by seeing an old friend when you walk into the room to audition for them, it will be a welcome surprise, not one filled with uneasy silence and dread.

3. You will also look around the room and get caught up watching other actors preparing their scene. It's an oddly captivating visual. I mention this because the waiting room is a vulnerable place. Seeing other actors' choices can lead to wrongly judging your own choices. Don't ever see something another actor is doing and try to do it better. More often than not, their ideas won't work for you, so stick to your plan.

And finally, there are times you can clearly hear someone else's audition going on while sitting in the waiting area. Tell the casting associate you'll be right outside, and go out. Every laugh or silence from inside the room can be grossly misinterpreted and do damage to your very fragile ego just before you audition.

What Do I Control in an Audition?

Three things: Being on time. Being prepared. Being polite.

1. *Be on time.* You will always wait, but you still have the responsibility to be there on time, for a few reasons. The casting director will love you for it. You will have more time to collect yourself and prepare your last thoughts on the scene, and you honor the contract you make with your agent, yourself, and the process. Do not undervalue that. Use this time to do the final part of your preparation, so you go in fresh and excited to act.

2. *Be prepared.* Put in all the time you know you need to realize the scene before you arrive. If you come across a word or scenario in the scene that you don't know, look it up. Don't take the easy way out and think you'll just ask when you get there. If you need the meaning and pronunciation of an obscure French word, call a French bakery and ask the owner to help you, or find a website that gives you the answer. The internet gives you almost no excuse to ask the writer for a definition of something he's written. Do you need an accent? Have it down cold. Don't wing it from memory. Go in looking like you are the most prepared, easiest to direct actor in the world.

Do you have to memorize the whole scene? Isn't being off book how you do your best work? Sometimes because of the late hour you received the text there is simply not enough time, but do your best to memorize at much as you can. At the minimum, get at least the first page memorized so you don't have to look at it for the first few beats when they're studying you the hardest. In lieu of being very quick at memorizing, you have to develop a smooth system of picking the lines off the page as you audition. Some people use a bright highlighter to see their lines, while others use their finger to keep track of where they are on the page. Looking down, picking up the line swiftly, and delivering it is accepted, but don't get caught reading the page. If you memorize the text, you should still hold the pages as you do the scene. It's a subtle reminder that this is still an audition, not the best work you can do. For theatre auditions, absolutely be off book and certainly show them your opening night performance.

3. *Be polite and friendly.* If there is one moment of being potentially phony that I'm going to endorse, it's this. When they ask (and they always do) "How are you?" your answer should always be a warm "Great!" or something like that. When they ask about another job or a director or your hometown, the answer should always be positive. Why? Idle chatter is part of every audition, because it's their feeling-out process. They want to know whether you are agreeable. Are you a tortured artist burdened with your own demons who might cost them time on the set? Are you someone they would simply want to be around for a week, or three months, or five seasons? It's their first encounter with you. They glean what they can from your answer to "How are you?" I'm not saying this has to be done with cheerleader-like enthusiasm. What I'm saying is that you can be yourself, but it's a very good idea to reveal only the happy positive side of yourself at this point. When you're answering a question, look at the person who asked it. It's easy to be distracted by the scene and dismiss the empty chatter. Take a moment to regard them, and then go to the scene when they make it clear they want you to read.

There are times when the room is all business and it's clear they simply want to watch you act and not chit chat. You can still give out positive vibes without forcing a conversation on them. Feel the vibe of the room and move forward with my advice in your head. Molly Hagan said it all when she said, "There are three things they can always smell on you when you walk into an audition: desperation, superiority and inferiority."

The Audition Itself

You should understand that appearance is a big, big part of this. Not so much in theater, but in movies and especially in TV, your looks are your biggest asset and hindrance. This shouldn't shock you too much since they call you in based on your headshot. You'd think that would mean the looks part of the competition is over, but your picture gave them only the parameters of your looks. Your in-person appearance gives them the rest.

I've been to auditions where the sign-in sheet included a section for height. What does that mean? It means they're height casting. Do you think if your height is enough of a concern to ask you about it before they've even seen you, that your reading is all that important?

So take a lot of the pressure off yourself by knowing that you will or will not pass what I call the threshold test. As you cross the threshold into the room, they'll decide whether you're physically right or not. There is nothing you can do here. You are what you are. You might be thinking right now, "But I can control how I look." You can't control that you're five feet tall. If you don't pass the threshold test, it won't be your day. You don't know it, but your stellar reading today is now about impressing them for the future. There is always the myth that your brilliance as an actor should overcome whatever physical mismatches you have with the role at hand. That has happened, but I can tell you it's not the rule. They look at physical types and then skills.

I mention this first because if you give a great audition, you *nail* it, and you don't get the job, you'll get stuck thinking you could have done more. Whereas it could have been nothing more than a physical expectation that stymied you. The danger here is that if you don't know that, you can start to overreach or push on your next auditions, trying to make up for that feeling of "What more can I do to get a job!? I'm doing my best!" You probably are, but not getting a job can be about something as simple as your haircut not being what they had in mind.

A while back I read a quote by an Oscar-winning actress who was asked how she felt about being cast in the roles she was in, up until her Oscar win. She said, "They don't look for an actress and ask her to dye her hair, they look for a blonde and see if she can act." True, and sad. The irony is that your God-given beauty can limit you in a business that's all about beauty.

Greeting the Room and Starting Your Reading

1. Don't shake anyone's hand unless someone reaches out to you. They see a lot of actors, and people are often sick. Don't assume you're being a good greeter by extending your hand and making them feel they must

meet you with theirs. Only move toward them if they move toward you. Acknowledge them from where you're standing if they don't.

2. Before you read they *always* ask you, "Any questions about the scene?" Don't ask any questions unless you're truly stumped. Do not start the audition with an apology. A question is an apology? It can feel that way. Let me explain.

General questions come across like an apology for the work you are about to do. I've been a reader in auditions many times and general questions from actresses about the character come across like you're saying, "I don't know what to do here." Of course you as an artist are trying to get the scene the best it can be by asking for a little guidance, but it's a very opposite feeling on the other side of the room. A question like, "Do you see this guy as funny?" is a general question that let's them know you're lost. You and your talent are thinking, "I can make this funny, or quite moving and sad, it depends on what they want." That's a question to ask before you get in the room. Have your agent call or ask one of the casting associates while you're in the waiting room. Now, I have heard some actors ask questions about specific moments and it did come across like they were quite ready and wanted to simply tweak one small moment tighter, but it was how they did it. It was a very specific question about a specific beat. So I say don't ever start with an apology. Do the scene the way you feel is right. If you've passed the threshold test and you're in the ball park character wise, they'll adjust any which way you might have strayed from their interpretation of the scene.

The two deadliest questions you can be asked before you start your reading are "What did you think of the script?" and "How old are you?" How do you handle them?

First the script issue. If you loved it, then it's easy—be honest. If you didn't, stick to the stock answer, "I loved it," or your own variation on that theme. If right now you're thinking, "But what if I didn't like it and I don't want to lie?" let me save you some embarrassment. You may think that this question is their way of testing your talent and seeing if you could find the flaws in the script by being that one very smart, very intuitive artist. Or maybe you want to expound on why the script doesn't totally work for you, but don't be fooled. They don't go into production with a script they are hoping some actor can fix during an audition. They ask you what you thought of their script because they're trying to find out whether you are of the same mind as they are.

So you don't love the script, but would happily do the job if you got it. Here's how you answer, "I loved how my character..." and you expound on the thing that you found in preparing for the scene that makes it fun or challenging for you. Be honestly enthusiastic about something. Don't worry about nailing down any conceptual, overall, thematic ideas behind the writing. Just be sure to compliment something with your answer.

If for some reason they hear your answer and persist with, "Yeah, but what do you really think of it?" then take this as an invitation to tell them what you thought of it without apology. Usually if they ask twice, they're looking for solid actors who can break down a character by instinct off the page.

"How old are you?" is something they're technically not allowed to ask you in the first place, but they sometimes do, and it's a dangerous thing to answer, as it helps them type you. If they are thinking you look twenty, why do they need to know you're actually twenty-six or seventeen? One reason they are asking could be because of labor laws concerning minors. Another could be that they want to know where they can put you in their heads for easy filing. It's a very touchy thing, because casting folks have to keep track of so many actors. If they know your real age is thirty, it helps them quickly decide whether or not to bring you in to audition for the twenty-five-year-old they're casting.

How do you answer? You really don't want to say, "It's illegal to ask me that." That's not going to make you any friends. Instead, you avoid it with a humorous response. "You know I can't tell you that. I'm an actor. I have no age." Funny, huh?

The answers they get most often are "I'm the age of the character" or "whatever age you need me to be," so don't use those. Try to find a fun way to say that it's uncomfortable answering that question. If they persist, the easy way out of it is to give them a generality—"I play early twenties" or "I'm in my mid thirties"—but be creatively, humorously, vague. Do your best to leave your age to their perception.

Once I had a job in a movie playing a father, and on day five of shooting the director casually asked me my age. When I told him, he was shocked that I was younger than he thought. His face told me he immediately thought he had miscast me. All through casting and the first days of shooting he had no problem seeing me as the father of this young boy. He was pleased with the father-son scenes that we had shot already. But from the moment he knew my real age, his direction became about how I wasn't playing the scene like a father. That hard number on my age became his focus, not what I was doing in the scene. The age game is sad, abusive, and weird, but it's real. Try not to get wrapped up in it.

Reading

You've started your reading. Except for theater auditions, you will almost always be reading with the casting director or someone from his office. They believe they give you your best opportunity to shine by doing absolutely nothing with their half of the scene. So you usually have to act in a vacuum. They usually don't color their words much above a monotone and have no strong interpretation of the scene. There are a myriad of books and workshops for dealing with this hurdle. Consider this until you find something that works best for you. Endow the reader with how you think the scene should go. When she speaks to you, respond with how your mind says the line just sounded, not from what you really just heard. Because if you work off what the reader gives you, your reading will surely end up looking like you're a breath away from a coma.

There will always be a video camera in the audition. Don't play to the camera; do the scene with the reader. If news of the taping has you thinking about doing your makeup differently, usually the lighting is so average your day makeup will suffice, but you'll learn that as you go. There are also many classes for "on camera auditioning." I don't know what you need to do differently when auditioning with a reader versus auditioning with a reader while a camera records it. I guess there are tricks you can use to make yourself look good later during the playback. I won't speak to that as I'm unaware of the techniques, but if you feel completely insecure about auditioning for a camera, it might be worth your time to find out about them just to quell your fears.

Is it ever okay to stop your reading and start over? If you stumble over the first few words and need to straighten yourself out, that's okay. Stop, sort yourself out, and ask to start again. Usually just getting the words out once makes saying them again easier. So take a beat and ask to start again. No big deal.

If the reader or anyone else in the room does something that throws you and you know it hurt your reading, stop and ask to do that section again. Usually they will stop and apologize and tell you to do it again. It's your scene, so get the most out of it.

If you truly see something new in the words that you didn't before, it's okay to stop. But this is a huge pet peeve of every casting director, so you have to be sure that you have a very fresh way to do the scene. If you do the scene the same way after asking for a new start, you will be seen as someone who has wasted their time. They will be very indignant toward the actor who thinks that by giving the same reading twice he's going to have a better shot at getting the job.

This leads us to the next issue that can come up during your reading.

What do you do about that sinking feeling that the whole thing is going really badly? Nothing. You finish, without apology, and go. Most of the time you are wrong about how bad it was. You hold your head up, thank them, and leave. Think about when a skater in the Olympics does a fair routine and hangs her head at the end. Doesn't it tell us all she knows she sucked? Just keep moving, go get a cup of tea with a friend, or go work out. You may feel the real thing to do is to look at them when you're done and say, "I've done much better," or some comment that lets them know that you know this was bad work, but don't.

That admission comes across only as a real lack of confidence in your talent, not your reading. A friend of mine once tanked a reading for a big director on a big film. He had that bad feeling that despite his efforts to knock it out of the park, it just fell flat. So in the awkward silence that followed his reading he casually said, "It was better at home," and the director replied, "It always is." My friend felt horrible the rest of the day. Leave your reading alone and get out. There will be more days of perfect auditions and more days of awful auditions—that's the way it is when you are an artist.

We are not machines that can replicate a performance in exacting specifications. Leave your reading alone and get out.

I've Finished My Reading

There is always a silence that follows your reading that feels weird to just let hang. Let it hang. Every move you make is being watched. Don't undermine your reading with a comment or clever remark that's got nothing to do with anything but filling a slightly uncomfortable void of time. Don't say "scene." They will say thank you. You will smile and say thank you and then you will get out because anything you say right after your reading about your reading looks like an apology for what you just did. Don't ever ask, "Do you want to see anything else?" In your mind you might be discussing your reading like an actor in rehearsal would, but it looks like insecurity. Remember, very few people in this business have your knowledge of acting or theater. Your process is lost on them. If they want you to do anything but get out, they'll let you know. Don't ask.

Actors look so much more confident when they simply do their work and leave. You get your three minutes and everything else is their time. You will have so much more impact if your choices and execution of the scene fill the room with your spirit than if you try to talk them into liking you. Let your audition speak for you.

To summarize: go in, read, and gracefully leave.

Everything Went Well Until I Began to Talk

First, count yourself lucky to have an audition in the first place. Many, many, many actors don't. It's easy to lose sight of the basic blessing—you had an opportunity. Next, know that you have no real idea how you affected the people in the room. I don't know an actor alive who hasn't been shocked to get a job because he was sure he just bludgeoned the reading. You don't really know and you can't really know.

You just had a bad day and didn't execute your plan well and it felt awful. You know you're better than that. Count yourself as human. No big deal. You might not be getting a paycheck from that show, but that's the game too. Take some mental notes about what, if anything, was missing from your preparation and log it away and then try again.

Here are some things I have learned along the way from the bad-day auditions.

1. I was off because the material wasn't ready. I have been in the room *many* times and had the writer say, "You know what? The scene doesn't work. Skip it, do the next one." Now what are all the other actors that were in before me thinking? They sucked, and they didn't nail the scene, *but* by the writer's admission, the scene was poorly written and thus "un-nailable." Does the casting director call all the previous actors back in to do it again? Does he call them at home to let them know that it was the fault of the writing and not that they

can't act? No, those actors are left to beat themselves up. So understand that the material may be to blame.

2. The room was shut down to me because they already had who they wanted. You can feel it when the room is looking at you to be a solution. You can also feel it when they're not.

3. They were uninterested because I didn't pass the threshold test.

All these reasons point to one thing: You have to use your time wisely. If you don't get hired you have to use each audition to learn more about yourself and get better at acting in a vacuum. Don't use the time to tell yourself that you have two more months and then you're done. Don't use it to tell yourself that it's all your fault. Every time you go in for an audition, go in for yourself and try to do a great job acting under the circumstances you are given. This practice will keep you looking at the next audition for the challenge you can rise to, rather than approaching it with dread.

I can't give you a sure-fire formula for success, but I can give you a formula for failure: try to please everybody all the time.

—Herbert Bayard Swope,
Pulitzer Prize-winning journalist

The Callback

Think of how hard it would be for you to see thirty, fifty, or seventy-five people do the same scene and remember them all very specifically. Yes, they have a video tape to look over, but in making the choice of who to hang their career on, they always want to watch a live actress again. That is the reason for the callback. It's good news for you. You get another chance to go show off what you're made of. They are thinning the herd for the entrance of the next level of executive decision makers. With each callback more executives will be in the room, which gives you many more chances to panic and endow them with absolute rule over your self worth. Watch out for that.

Callbacks can sometimes feel like a system designed to have us back in so we can self destruct. Like they are calling you back only to see if you were a fluke the first time. It's so much more daunting to have a callback than just an audition because it means you are one step closer and more is at stake. That's how it feels, but it's not the truth.

The material and the craft of acting haven't changed. What you can control hasn't changed. The only thing that has changed is your perception. The work is the same as the first time, but our minds, and our agents' enthusiasm, make it feel like there is a much bigger burden on our talent. Please don't fall prey to this. Acting is acting. Pressure is self induced.

Callbacks have a way of throwing us into doubt about our abilities to nail a piece more than once. This is just our fear at play and it's silly. When you do a play, you do the same scenes night after night. You don't stand in the wings every night and say, "Oh my God, how am I going to do this again?" You just go on and do it again. An audition isn't like a play. In a play your focus is on the other actors and the task at hand in each scene. In an audition your focus is on yourself, because everyone's focus is on you too. Every move you make is so scrutinized that the process feels like it's make or break with every syllable. It will be that way only if you let it. Remember, your job is to act and to relinquish what you don't have control over.

A rule of thumb is to keep your head out of the other team's play book. Don't waste time thinking about why they want to see you again or who else was called back or anything else that deals with trying to enter the mind of the producer. It's nothing more than a distraction from the most important thing you can control—your work. It's their ball, their court, and their insanity. Leave their issues to them. If you start your callback trying to second guess the guessers, you're relinquishing an opportunity to do good work, for the opportunity to get caught up in gossip and hearsay. Do not get distracted.

Do I try to copy what I did in my first audition? This is a common question. Then comes the thought, "If I'm going to duplicate it, what exactly did I do?" Don't worry about matching your last performance exactly. The easiest way to accomplish that is to prepare the same way you did for your initial audition. Go through the same process, act with the same freedom you had the first time, and odds are you'll do about the same thing. You'll also be free with it, fresh in your execution, not tight and trying to mimic yourself from a week ago, which is the sign of a rookie. You will often hear from your agent, "They loved you! Go back in there and do exactly what you did the first time and I'm sure you're gonna get it!" However, you never want to act with the tension of trying to duplicate a previous performance.

Sometimes adjustment notes or additional pages are added to the callback appointment. Great, more to do! Go through your process the same way you would if it was a first audition. Don't think you've got to somehow merge the two separate ideas of the original audition with new pages or notes. Any notes right now are taken with a higher sensitivity, but it's just a note. It's just another scene to work on. Roll the whole thing over in your mind like you have the freedom to find something new in it.

What if I see another way of portraying the character? That happens, but you don't want your interpretation to stray too far from your initial reaction to the material. They are calling you back based on what you did with their script the first time. Try to reinforce those ideas. If they want anything different they'll send notes.

There is a rule of thumb that says you should wear the same thing to your callback that you wore to the audition. It's a superstition maybe, but it's probably a good idea in that it will eliminate one decision that day. If you don't remember what you wore, don't sweat it.

So, what do the executives, directors, or producers want in a callback? They want to see if you're consistent with your acting. They want to see if you're as pretty as they remember, or as edgy, or as quirky. They want to see if you're as fun and agreeable as you were the first time. They want to see if they can get everyone in the room to decide on any of the ten people they have brought back in order to go on to the next callback. They want to see if you crack under pressure, but mostly, they are all sitting there hoping that the actors they've brought please their boss enough to have him choose a cast that can now shoot the show or movie. That's how they keep their jobs. You'd be surprised how many times a casting session ends with the big boss choosing no one.

The room has its own tension; don't bring any more to it. You can remain cool because you know what your job is and you're not worried about the fact that last year's Miss America was also called back. You're an actress, so act. Stay clear on what you can control and what is just a distraction or fear creeping in. Make the finish line the next line of the scene, and not the million dollars you'll make in season five.

Do Audition Seminars Help?

If you have no skill at auditioning, a seminar that gives you some tools would be worthwhile. I've never taken one—I just developed my own way. But surely a good class would accelerate your learning curve. I do think it's possible to get good at acting off the page simply by practicing. A class is always a budgetary issue.

In Summary

Auditioning has taken on the reputation of being a big pain in the ass. Very few actors like or look forward to auditions, but I believe that's because actors wrongly see them as a barrier. The process isn't going away anytime soon, so it's my advice to see them as an opportunity to show off and give yourself over to the folks in the room. Give them whatever piece of you the material calls for and you'll be doing your job. If you do your job, the acting gods will smile on you and you'll soon be getting paid to get better. Fulfillment is about the best feeling an artist can know. Doing good work with people you like while paying your bills—it's the only fulfillment we really get.

You've Booked a Job!

How do you piss off an actor?

Give him work.

WHEN YOU GET A JOB, YOU will need good working habits. I'll outline a few here. These will keep you in good stead until you make your own, but first a few other things.

The Imposter Syndrome

If right after you booked a highly sought after job, you get struck sharply by the realization that you really don't know what you're doing and they were wrong to hire you, you should know that you're right on track! It seems to happen to everyone, and not just on the first job either. It stays with you. It's the feeling that you're sure they have made a mistake hiring you and you'll be found out when you actually go to do the part. This all happens because you care about what you're doing and you have something at stake, namely your reputation. It's normal and part of your learning curve. What do you do to get through it? You go do the job. Tell yourself you're going to get there and check in with the A.D. (assistant director), then take the rest minute by minute.

If you get a TV spot, ask your agent to put in your contract that you get a copy of the show as part of your pay. You'll want this to add to your reel. Not every show will do it, but it's worth the request. There was a time when if you asked, any show would make you a dupe without a problem, but economics are such that they now want up to $75 to make you a copy. So ask your agent to see what they can do. You may not get it, but you have a better shot at getting it up front when they need you rather than after, when their minds are on the next show. Yes you can record it off the TV, but a production copy is always cleaner and makes your demo reel look better.

Going to Work

Usually the first person to contact you from the show is the costume designer or someone from the wardrobe department. The people who work in the wardrobe department are costumers. What they handle—your clothing for the show—is wardrobe. The designer's assistant that handles the running of the clothing on set is the wardrobe supervisor. Do not call them wardrobe-ers, even though they say, "I'm calling from wardrobe." If you can't remember someone's name on the set you ask, "Are you from the wardrobe department?" or "Is someone from the wardrobe department here?" or "Is the costume designer available?" Stay away from "Wardrobe! I need help here." They know that your comfort is in the difference between 15 1/2 inches and 16 inches in your collar. They are very exacting about their trade. You'll show them that you respect that by being exacting about how you refer to them and what they do.

When someone from the wardrobe department calls, they are calling to get your sizes so they can start putting your clothing options together. They are not the people to talk to about your overall ideas for the character, nor your feeling for the script, or your scheduling problems. Just talk about what they called you for. You *must* give them your sizes accurately! Whatever your fear about your body, they don't care or judge. They do care if your ego sends them shopping for size 6 clothes to fit your size 10 body. So you will give them your real, today sizes. Don't be coy and tell them your whole body building story and how some days you're a 56 chest but some days you're a 52. They have heard everyone's body image neurosis; just give them your sizes.

If you don't really know your sizes because it's your first job, then say as much and they will probably have you come in for a measuring before the fitting. When you get your sizes from them, write them down and keep them for future jobs.

They may ask you to bring some of your own clothes in to the fitting because they want something broken in or better fitting than they can provide. It's no big deal. If you're uncomfortable with it, just say you don't have anything like that. Be polite about it. Wearing your own shoes is something you might want to consider as you may be standing for long stretches. You don't necessarily want some brand new, or worse, very old shoes on your feet all day. You can always bring your most comfy, appropriate pair to the fitting and show them to the designer, saying, "These are really comfy for me. Would you consider using these?"

When dealing with your fitting and the wardrobe department staff, you are dealing with the entire production crew. Your conduct on the phone and in person during this first point of contact with the crew will be passed on to anyone and everyone, from the caterer to the casting department. The crew is like any other family or group that lives together for long hours every day. They need new subjects to talk about to fill up the hours together, so they talk all day long about whatever's going on. Again, who doesn't like gossip? Be very cordial, helpful, and thankful to them. Compliment the clothing choices and discuss your clothing ideas or needs with them early on. Never make them look stupid, even if you are right. The wardrobe, hair, and makeup departments make your life easy on set. If they resent you, your days will be long.

At the Fitting

First and foremost among complaints from costume designers is bad hygiene. They are seeing you undress and slap on many sets of clothing—the last thing they need is the sticky somebody who just worked out and ran over to do a quick fitting. It sends them a message of disrespect and it makes their work harder. It will also start the gossip about you moving around the set before you get there. Even if you're going for the rebel persona, don't make folks suffer. Grab a shower before the fitting. Also, always wear undergarments—this goes for both genders. Costume designers get disgusted by the lack of respect one shows them by doing a fitting in the nude. They have to return most of the clothing from the fitting, so don't make it harder for them.

Consider that the photos they take of you in your wardrobe fitting will be distributed all the way up the chain of command. So if you go in raw and unkempt, the same people you dolled up to impress with your looks at the audition will now have this unflattering view of you. Not to mention that a studio executive might be seeing you for the first time. It's an opportunity for someone to form a bad opinion of your looks that you don't have to give them. No, you don't have to do full camera ready make-up, but put some thought into how you will look in those pictures. And always smile in the pictures. Why? You'll see when you get to the "Nightmares" section.

Finally, respect your wardrobe items. Don't throw your wardrobe around during the day. Don't wear it to lunch and drip on it, thinking that someone will clean it later, and never leave your wardrobe in a pile on the floor at the end of the day. Hang your clothes back up the same way they were delivered to you. You will be known as a class act if you do this, and you will get very good service from the wardrobe department.

The Clothing

If you want to keep your wardrobe, don't steal it, or think you can. They can withhold your paycheck until they get it back. The way to try to get it is to ask the designer if you can buy it. If they can sell it, they will sell it at half their price to you, which is usually pretty cheap. Sometimes, they have to hang on to clothing to build their inventory, and you have to settle for a no.

They are very aware that everyone wants to steal their clothes, and part of their job is being accountable for them. Don't start out your career being a pain for the wardrobe department. It may feel like it gives you a fun or rebellious reputation, but somewhere along the way it will backfire, and you will feel stupid for having done it. Approach the designer and say, "I don't think I've ever looked this good in clothing! Is there a chance I could buy this when I'm done?" This compliments their work and let's them know exactly which clothes you are interested in. Then if you treat them well during the shoot, they often hand you things you liked when you wrap. They have ways of making things happen for you if you're at least up front with them about it. I was once a guest star on a very popular TV show where the designer talked about a vacation she was taking. I gave her copious notes on the very place she was going because it was a place I had gone many times. At the end of the week the designer called me in my dressing room and said "What do you want to keep?" I got two very pricey items and I didn't have to ask. They know everyone wants free or discounted new clothes. Don't get sneaky and think they won't be on to you.

The Next Phone Call

The second call you usually get when you book a job is from the second A.D. with your call time. Whatever phone numbers he gives you, write them down and keep them with you until you arrive at work. If your car breaks down en route to the job, your first call is to the second A.D., even before road service. If they leave your call time and location on your voice mail, whether they ask for it or not, call them back to confirm that you have all your information.

When you call them back do not ask, "When will I be done?" You can ask directions, what scenes are slated for the day, the order in which the scenes will be shot (but that can change), and where you are supposed to park or be met. However, do not start your relationship with the set by asking how long until you are done with them.

Usually the night before a call sheet is delivered to you, listing the next day's work and the location, with directions and parking instructions, but not always.

While you are on the phone with the second A.D. be sure to treat him with the attitude "How can I make your job easier where I'm concerned?" not "You work for me, I'm the talent." Believe me, they hear things like

"Will there be fat free craft service, because I'm on a low fat diet?" from actors all the time, when they are just trying to get you updated on your work day. If your need is dire and can't be avoided (like a medical issue) say, "Who's the best person to talk to about my lactose intolerance for the scene where I have to drink milk?" It gives them the option to send you directly to the person best suited to handle your issue. That's a help to them, because the A.D. generally handles everything on the set, so any request you make, they will have to handle. But if they feel like you're not just trying to be pampered, and you're willing to do the leg work concerning your issue, they will know you're not a diva and that you're responsible for your own needs. It'll also make them want to solve the issue for you quickly.

If you do have some pressing time issue during a job, your agent is the one who should bring it to the attention of the production, and preferably when the booking is taking place. Last minute conflicts do arise, but unless you're on very good terms with the producers, asking for special attention concerning a time conflict during a shooting day is best left to your agent. Do your best to never bring a time issue up with the first A.D. or director. Why? It's another bad habit actors are famous for and it makes the crew and director crazy. In their eyes we have the easiest job with the easiest hours and all we do is complain about them. The crew despises the bitching actor who's checking his watch. They will have started that day long before you and will be there long after you. Always look like you're in it for as long as it takes, without any problems. Actors start with the diva stereotype, so don't add to it. Let your agent deal with problems you have on the set.

Bringing friends with you to work on the first day is a no-no. People can usually visit at some point, but go see how it feels on the set first, and be sure to ask the first A.D., "What's the protocol on bringing someone with me to work here?" Some sets are very prickly about outsiders, especially sets with major stars, or feature films where they are trying to protect the content of the movie. They protect their privacy and the ability for the set to be a place of work, not for gawkers. Wives and husbands are usually okay anytime, but do your first day alone for sure.

The A.D.s are your link to a happy set life. There are usually three of them—first, second, and second second. After that there is sometimes a third, but usually they just have legions of P.A.s—production assistants. They schedule your call time in to the set and they can work the scenes to get you out early. They schedule everything, and if you're a bitchy actor they have ways of making your world a whole lot tougher without it ever looking like they're doing it. Conversely, they will bend over backwards for the actor that makes their job easier. So, to be good to your assistant directors, always be easy to find. That doesn't mean you have to quietly sit on the set within eyesight (although they love that). It means that whenever you go somewhere around, off, or near the set, go to someone in the A.D. department and gently tell them, "I'm going to my car for a second. I'll be back in my room in ten minutes." Now they know where to look for you. Or better, "I'm going to the phone. I'll swing by and wave to you on my way back to my room." You don't interrupt the set to do this and it tells them you are considerate of their job. The worst thing that can happen to an A.D. is to have the director call for you and he has to say, "We can't find her." The A.D. looks stupid if they "lose" an actor. It creates downtime on the set. Time is money. If you get lost just once you will quickly find yourself being baby-sat or confined to a few areas. A.D.s are smart. They will insure that they won't look bad and the set will not lose shooting time again.

If you're responsible and respectful of their needs you'll be allowed to go wherever you want to kill time while you wait for your scene to be shot. It will make your work day nicer, especially if you're in a great location. Because I earned the A.D.'s trust, I was handed a walkie-talkie and told, "Listen for your name and hustle back." This afforded me hours of roaming around, instead of sitting in a trailer going stir crazy.

Never complain about the wait. Occasionally an A.D. or someone from production will apologize for how long it's taking to get you "up" (on set). They love when you say (and you will say), "No problem, I'm yours all day."

You will wait hours for the simplest of shots. Your job is to wait, and to wait patiently. It's very easy to get nuts after a few hours. Remind yourself that you could be using this time to pick up another shift at the restaurant or sit at home unemployed watching the TV, bitter about the bad actors who are working. Remember, you get paid to wait, you work for free. It's not the other way around. So when you are sitting on set waiting, say, "I'm being paid to read this book / learn my lines / write letters. How great is this?!"

Handle grievances nicely. You may go into "meal penalty" (when they don't feed you by the allotted time according to SAG contracts), or a "forced call" (when they ask you to return to work earlier than SAG allows), or overtime, or some other contract violation while shooting. A.D.s hate the whistle-blowing actor. They know the rules very well. They know when they are breaking them. They are usually breaking them because their boss has told them to. It is best to have your agent bring it up with the producers, but if it's something you feel you need to address right then and there you will do it with the knowledge that the A.D. isn't trying to take advantage of you.

You might see other actors pushing an infraction issue with an A.D. That's because actors get paid for these infractions, and it can be a nice chunk of change. Don't join the fight. If the A.D. is aware of it, you'll all get the penalty fee. If the A.D. is going to fight the infraction, no need to make an enemy of him. I'm not saying to remain quiet about abuse. I'm saying that many times these penalties are over being a minute or two late for something. A.D.s are usually very fair, but if you must speak up, speak up. You and the A.D. will find a way to deal with it.

An A.D. will also need to sign you out at the end of the day, so make yourself easy to find, or better yet, find them and say, "I'm going to change and then I'll find you to sign out, okay?" They almost always find you sooner, but it's a nice way of letting them know you are going to help them wrap you out (sign you out). Do check to see that the time on the sign out sheet is right. If it's way off, it is okay to ask, "Why does this say 8 pm? It's 10 right now." If they don't change it or give you an answer that makes sense, leave it alone. Call your agent about the problem; don't argue it out with the A.D. right there.

This is something to remember about studio management. I was once owed several hundred dollars for a minor violation, and the studio admitted fault and then asked me if I'd take half the amount, letting me know that I'd be in their favor if I did. I said no, because our union fought to put these protections in place for just that reason. If they learn we will negotiate on a case by case fashion, they are sure to take liberties with our contracts.

On the Set

As you walk the set, never step or stand on cables.

When you are not in the scene that's being shot, always listen for "rolling" and "cut" to know when you can speak or walk. You never want to ruin a take because you didn't know they were shooting.

Never say, "Makeup!" or "Wardrobe!" Say instead, "Is there someone from the makeup, hair, or wardrobe department here?" or "Could I get a touch up please?" Whenever anyone touches you up (make up, hair) or straightens your shirt, which happens a lot, always say, "Thank you." They watch the scene through the director's monitor to make sure you always look your best.

Thanking them will insure you get their attention in scenes where maybe your character is not the focus.

Never engage with another actor in a bitch session on the set or within earshot of the set. If you really need to dish, go into a private dressing room or a secure, far away place. While on the set, keep the conversation about the show you're on upbeat or better yet, talk about other subjects. There are ears everywhere and as I said before, one simple, misplaced comment can create your reputation with the crew. I'm not trying to scare you into being something you're not, nor am I trying to make you uncomfortable on the set. I'm trying to educate you to the mistakes I've made and suggest that there are good and bad places to have a conversation about anything that has to do with the job you are on.

If you've never done a film or TV show, you'll be introduced to the idea of continuity. That means matching your movements from take to take so that when the editor tries to cut the different angles together, you're not looking right in take one, and left in take two. The script supervisor is the person on set whose job it is to look out for these types of things. So she may yell out to you, "You had the paper in your right hand last time!" You should never say, "Well that was last time, I'm trying something different this time!" If you do, you're announcing to the set that you've decided that all the previous takes are no good, because you're making them unusable by switching hands. Unless there is a concrete reason to change something, you'll need to match your movements from take to take. I'm not saying to match things robotically; I mean go through the same motions. If you honestly need to change something, consult the director. Don't just make continuity changes on your own.

Here are some random terms you may hear people say, and if you don't know what they mean, they may make you feel like a rookie.

On your mark or *Hit your mark.* Means please stand on the tape on the floor that is your mark. Marks are how the focus puller keeps you in focus, so hit them.

Final touches. All the departments step on the set to fix things right before they call "rolling!" That means hair and makeup folks coming at you too.

Turning around. They are done shooting the scene in the current direction and are now turning the camera and lights around to shoot the other direction (or on the other person) in the scene. This means a long break for you.

Moving in for coverage. They are going to shoot the scene tighter now, in close up.

The Marsha. (From the Brady Bunch, "Marsha, Marsha, Marsha.") The third to last shot of the day.

The Abby or Abby Singer. (After a director named Abby Singer, who became famous for calling the last shot of the day and having one more after that.) The second to last shot of that scene or of the day.

The martini. The last shot of the day.

Dollar days. This is an on-set lottery usually done at the end of the shooting week. A set P.A. collects dollars from everyone (with their name written on them) and at wrap, whoever's dollar is randomly picked out of the box wins the loot. This is a morale booster for the crew mostly, so the director, producer, and star usually drop bigger money in to make the winnings fat. The director, producer, and star can win, but it's seen as very cheesy if they take the money, so if their name is picked, they usually let it ride, or have another name picked out.

The Director

You may have met the director at the audition. Whatever happened at the audition may no longer be the case today, on the set, under the day's pressure, so take nothing for granted about how he may treat you during the shooting of your scene.

You surely don't have to treat him like he is god, but until you can get a feel for the mood of the set it's probably better to talk to him only about the work at hand. I say this because there is a tendency among actors to make a fan of the director in an effort to secure future work with your new best friend. Every director that ever directed knows this about actors. They can feel it when you're being just too interested in their coffee selection. Impress directors with your set savvy, your preparation, and your talent. They will always find a way to retain actors who make their shows and direction look good.

If you have an honest question about the lines or the meaning of the scene, that's all fair game. It helps to phrase it with something like, "Is this a good time to ask a question about my part?" This gives them the option to say, "In a minute" or "Later" without looking like they're putting off an eager actor.

When you want to suggest something to the director about the scene (which can be very touchy, especially on long running weekly TV shows that run like clockwork), use a phrase like, "Does it help you if I...?" Then the director has the opportunity to at least say, "Why?", at which time you can tell him your idea. If he says, "No," then we're all clear on how available he is to your input, and you can save yourself a harsher interaction with him. Always phrase your suggestions as if you are just trying to make the director's life easier. You'd be surprised how many actors say bluntly, "That doesn't work" or "This doesn't make sense. I should be over there, not here." This usually throws the director into ego mode, and then the set becomes a battleground about who's in charge, and is no longer about getting the best from the scene. Speaking politely to directors will allow them to direct you in a non-threatened way. They have seen plenty of young, eager actors who are going to reinvent the creative wheel with their massive talent. But you, the talented artist, who wants only the best for the scene, can sometimes speak quickly without knowing that it may be insulting an ego, and thus swiftly close the door on any good idea you might have had.

The Director of Photography and the Camera Operator

They are your best friends. Learn their names. They might not learn yours for a day or so—or never, if you're there for a heartbeat. I have been on sets where I was called "hey buddy" for days. When they are lining up shots, patiently listen to everything they say and move where they want you to. Say to them, "Is this good, Roger? What can I do to help?" or "Is this the right spot, or do you want me somewhere else?" They have a tough job, because protocol dictates that they don't speak to you directly about the movement they need—that is the director's job. It's about crossing the job description line and also not hitting actors from all sides with "direction." So you can help them by asking what they need, because if you're asking, they're not directing, they're just answering you. It's faster, they don't usurp the director, and they will love you for making it easier on them. You will suddenly get better lighting and the D.P. (director of photography) will kill any takes that don't flatter you. The D.P. is a great ally and usually one of the fun guys on the set too. If you listen closely, you will begin to learn the terms they use to communicate with each other. Don't be afraid to use them or ask what they mean so you can communicate easier.

When starting a take, don't mess with the "sticks" (the slate) when the camera assistant claps them to start the scene. It's usually fun to do, but if it messes up the slate and they have to "second stick," you look like a clown that's costing them time. Leave them alone.

Lunch

Sometimes you will be told you have a "walk away" lunch, which means you are on your own to buy your own lunch. You can ask the A.D. about the available eating options. Usually lunch is catered, but if it is a walk away lunch, be sure you know what time you are expected back.

When lunch is catered, the lunch protocol is that actors go to the front of the lunch line. This is because they must get back into hair and makeup for touchups before shooting can resume after lunch. So just go to the front of the line. Usually someone from the A.D. department is steering actors to the front anyway; the crew all understand this. You won't make any enemies by jumping the line.

Always tell the caterer that everything looks so good and it's hard to choose. Be polite with them, since they always have to feed many people in record time. Anything that makes the day nicer is always welcomed. You'll see how a few days of well spoken compliments turn into special treatment for you at meal time.

Wrap

At the end of the day, or your work for the day, thank crew people separately and quietly. Never yell a "Thanks everyone!" to the set. Make a quick walk around to the lighting guys (gaffer and grips), the camera guys, the A.D.s, and the whole set for a quick, honest, simple handshake and a "Thanks for today, you made it easy." I'm not suggesting you hunt every person down, but shake as many hands as you can on your way off the set and thank them personally. The crew never gets that from actors. Your next day on set or the next time you work with anyone from that crew, you will get better set treatment. Crew members are usually busy setting up the next shot or wrapping the night up, but they will always take a second to be thanked even if you have never spoken to them until then.

Bizarre Set Syndromes

Keep in mind that while you're on the set, quite often you will hear acting advice from everyone. *Everyone.* You might hear how the dailies from a scene other than yours looked "unbelievable." You might hear how *great!* the other actors are. Every person will have an opinion about the quality of acting—yesterday's, last week's, or their last movie's. You can't help but want these people to be impressed with you, to talk about how good you are. That's human.

Everyone Knows How to Act

You can never tell the hairdresser how to do hair.
You can never tell the make up person how to do make up.
You can never tell the costume designer how to design your wardrobe.
You can never tell the producer how to produce a movie.
You can never tell the sound department how to record dialog.
You can never tell the D.P. how to shoot or light.
You can never tell the director how to direct.
You can never tell the grips how to set light.
But they all feel free to tell you how to act!

I've discovered this to be true about the pride and egos of the various people on the set. They take great offense at the actor who criticizes their expertise, but it's funny how casually they discuss the efforts of the actors around them. It's a good idea to ignore everything they say about other actors, other scenes, and your work. It's nice to hear compliments of course, but it's funny how sometimes you can find yourself competing for the set's approval. It's a dangerous game—stay out of it.

There is also something that happens to actors when they are working that I call *sudden entitlement syndrome* or *the diva syndrome*. This occurs when you get on a set and suddenly copious amounts of attention are being paid to you and every part of what you're doing that day. The props, your hair, the shirt you're wearing, everything about you is being discussed in detail. You're being asked questions you've never been asked before and being catered to like you've never been catered to before. This is happening because the production team is always trying to head off problems before you get to the set, to limit down time. All this dialog and focus on you alerts your ego to how critical your character and your comfort are to the production. It becomes easy to forget that just a week earlier you were praying for the audition. Even low budget sets are a luxury compared to unemployment.

So, with all that attention you start to believe you are super-worthy. Then you impose your every whimsical demand on the crew in the name of creating that place where the acting magic happens. This is where the spoiled actor stereotype is born. When the actor who is used to being treated like a pariah is suddenly dropped into a place where their every emotion, every turn, every phrase spoken is observed, applauded, and dare I say it, necessary, you can see how this syndrome can develop quickly.

I once did a TV show that shot at the beach, and on the beach was a large muscled show-off who made sure he got the attention of the A.D. He was recruited to be a background player for the day. The next day the director hired him for a non-speaking role because he was the right look for the threatening henchman. He was thrilled. He was now in a featured non-speaking role on a TV show, all from going to the beach and taking off his shirt. He went from $40/day as an extra to something like $125/day as a featured extra. The very next day he told the costume designer he didn't like the shirt she gave him to wear and chose something else for himself. The designer, frantically following him with the correct shirt, tried to explain he had to wear the same shirt because we were matching scenes from the previous day—that if he didn't wear the same shirt when the show aired he'd suddenly be in a different shirt in the middle of the scene. He flat refused with "I'm cool man, I like this shirt. Don't worry about it."

My co-star, another veteran of the business, looked over at this guy and said, "Hey hot-shot! Two days ago you were standing around on the beach—now your trailer is too small. Put the shirt on!" The guy was so embarrassed, he immediately changed his shirt. The costume designer breathed a sigh of relief and thanked my co-star. That summed up the whole phenomenon for me. My actor friend was succinct and correct.

How do you combat diva syndrome? How do you know where the line is between really having your acting needs met and not indulging your diva? You listen. You listen to yourself and ask yourself, would I stand for this kind of treatment from someone else? Would I rehire someone who was talking to me like this? Because that may be what you are losing sight of—the fact that every job ends. It's really funny how the set becomes the whole universe, a universe that will never end. But it always does. So has your behavior been worthy of a being rehired? If your answer to that question is in any way defensive, you probably have some fixing to do on the set. If there is one thing that is absolutely true about your acting career, it's this: you are only as good as your next job. Take care of the job you are on properly, and it will help you get to your next job. Consider this: personal character is defined by how you treat the people that you don't need anything from.

When You See the Finished Product

I want to make you aware of the potential shock of editing. The difference between how you remember the scene playing during shooting and what the editor or director does with it for the final cut can be very startling. By removing pauses in your dialog the editing may take your performance from looking thoughtful to looking anxious. The editor may also remove some of your lines or cut to a reaction shot of someone else in the scene during your lines. The worst of these, of course, is having whole scenes cut. Your first thought is usually that they didn't like your performance, and you can get insecure, but don't. Generally editing is just about dealing with the length of the show or movie. Sometimes it's because they have changed what they think the scene is about, so they find a way to use what they have to get their new point across. If they didn't like your performance, they would have kept shooting while you were on the set. Directors don't get to be directors by getting into editing and finding out they have no useable performances.

Also understand that if they didn't use part of your performance that you thought was special, it's almost always because they had to deal with a technical issue, not because you misjudged your performance. This is where the continuity issue I discussed before often comes into play. If you don't match, even though the take is brilliant, they can't use it. Every actor I know has a story about having one of their favorite moments cut out of something and thinking, "I must not be a good judge of my work—they cut what I thought was my best work in the film!" Usually if it's magic for you, it's magic for everyone, but it wasn't useable.

This is another "Don't take it personally' issue. If you do, you will find yourself spending a lot of time telling people how the scene should have looked, but how bad it was because of how they edited it. By the way, that's really boring for people to hear. It also makes you bitter. Leave the editing to the editing team. Be proud you were in something people are talking about and leave the discussion about how you should have looked out of it. It will also keep you doing good work on every take, not living for one brilliant take that they should use.

Advice

Why doesn't an actor look out the window when he wakes up?

Because then he wouldn't have anything to do that afternoon.

THE BIGGEST KILLER OF YOUR spirit will be the inclination to compare yourself, your work, and your career development to others. It's a foolish, degrading, and harmful thing to do to the artist within you, but isn't it our nature? Being raised in schools that rate us as A, B, and C students, or watching the Olympic commentators who ask the silver medalist about their disappointment with only winning silver, we get programmed early to think that the only value is winning the big prize. So we compare prizes to know how we fit into the hierarchy of the room, or the agency, or the theatre company. This is where a great deal of destructive thinking takes place, because art is subjective. It has no scale to be measured by. So while the choice of players for the best team a college football program can put on the field is decided by a stopwatch and drills, the play at the college drama department is always going to be cast by way of the director's opinion of who has talent and who doesn't. You could argue that it's an educated opinion, but there are no facts on which to rely. Aren't we then trying to use the wrong scale to compare ourselves and our progress?

Envy is the ulcer of the soul.

—Socrates

It's better to make a growth chart based on your personal growth rather than one that matches you up against the progress of other actors. I don't mean to say you should actually draw up a chart. You should keep a notebook of your appointments, calls, contacts, but I'm talking about the mental growth chart your mind runs through every day. To really mark your progress, keep your thoughts on where you were this time last year or last month. That way you will be able to feel good or disappointed based on what you are doing for yourself and not based on what some other actor has accomplished. I will fill you in on something here—every actor I know, famous or not, feels insecure about their position in the business. Consider that Montgomery

Clift, Alfred Hitchcock, and James Dean never won Oscars. Couldn't you then make the case that their work didn't really measure up? But Cher has won an Oscar, so I guess that means on her growth chart she's a much better artist than the other three people I named.

There is also the "phenom theory." Orson Welles created Hollywood's consensus masterpiece, *Citizen Kane* (which didn't win Best Picture), at twenty-three. If you haven't made a masterpiece by then, well, you must be simply mediocre. Charles "Yardbird" Parker, who is credited with birthing jazz, died at thirty-four. So if you're not a major influence by then, you could easily tell yourself it's not going to happen.

Billy Bob Thornton made *Sling Blade* at forty, and it's easy to say that his homemade project did more for his career than anything else he did. If you try to compare yourself to any star or acting classmate, you will surely find days in which you are elated at your progress and days where you just don't understand how so-and-so is in four movies and has never even been to an acting class! (Remember our hype chapter.) As a rule, compare yourself to yourself. A friend from acting school who got into a Broadway show just a few months after we graduated said to me, "We're all on different calendars." If you're not in this for the long haul, then maybe your lesson is that this is a fact-finding mission and you only want acting to work in the short term. Good! Now you know. So move forward with this understanding.

To live a creative life, we must lose our fear of being wrong.

—Joseph Chilton Pearce

The next piece of advice is about combating the congestion of spirit that comes from pursuing work. How do you keep your artist feeling healthy all the time? My advice? Accept inspiration wherever you can. Allow your soul to flourish. What separates artists from civilians is that we accept our inspiration and channel it into our work. It helps us get to know ourselves better and grow. Allowing new things to speak to you and influence your sense of the world and your art is a tool that will help guide you through the doldrums of auditions and rehearsals. Do your best not to shape, contort, or manufacture this gift. Just allow it, whatever it is—the cheesy song, the wildly off-beat poster, the cold day's walk, the short order cook who moves with total efficiency—real inspiration can be found anywhere if you allow it. Don't judge it or stop it. Let it wash over you for that brief or long moment and let it inform you once again why the arts chose you. After all, we want the inspiration, we need it, but for some reason we stifle it. Allow the free flowing inspiring events of your day to reaffirm your spirit.

We're actors—we're the opposite of people.

—Tom Stoppard

Practical Advice for the Process

1. *Honor your day job.* Don't numb yourself into thinking it's a separate part of your actor's life. It isn't. What better way to confirm your commitment to your artist than to do a meaningless job that allows you to go on pursuing your dream of an acting career? How else do you know you really want anything if you have no trials in the process? Every day you go in you are saying, "I want to be a working actress so badly that I will stay in this town and do this job until I can earn my living as an actress." That's a nice affirmation. Take pride in your commitment.

2. *Perform a career activity each day.* Long bouts of acting unemployment can cause a feeling of futility to creep in your psyche. So commit to doing at least one thing every day that is about advancing your career—a purely career-focused effort in addition to going to your day job. Read a play to make yourself more theatre literate or watch the movie of a director you may meet if the audition comes through. Make sure your agent has enough headshots. Do at least one thing each day to remind yourself that your career isn't on autopilot. It also helps you to fight the feeling that you're always waiting on someone else.

I merely took the energy it takes to pout and wrote some blues.

—Duke Ellington

3. *Strike a balance in your life.* Have a significant positive alternative for fulfillment through a non-paying job, a charity that means a lot to you, or a job that requires that you engage in it with the best you've got. Relying on the business of acting as your sole source of joy will surely leave you less than joyful most of the time. Acting brings joy, but the business of getting acting work is a fairly routine grind. Having something else that really engages you will allow acting to be part of your life, not the emotional center of it. Until such a time when acting really does fill your entire day, I think you'll do yourself a favor to have your mind occupied by another endeavor that feels good and feeds your soul. You can drone through your day job and still honor it.

I mention this because I've learned that it's an odd phenomenon that when you set up your whole day around (cue the horror-film music) *the audition,* you do nothing but think about it, prepare for it, and wait for it. Then you usually arrive late, your reading falls flat, and nothing goes right. Somehow when an audition is simply a part of your day, your preparation is more focused, you make sharper choices, and you arrive on time. Making the audition a part of your day allows the enormity of the opportunity to take on its proper significance. No one should spend twenty-four hours straight working on one page of TV dialogue, but if it's the only thing you have to focus on for two days, you will. This isn't a way to trick yourself into being calm at an audition. It's about perspective and balance. Balance is everything.

4. *Seek other artistic endeavors.* On the days you might be feeling especially low, do something creative besides acting to motivate and inspire your artist and to get you out of the house. Go to a museum, seek out a painting that intrigues you, and instead of simply appreciating the finished product, try to imagine the artist painting it and what they looked like working on the canvas.

Paint your own canvas for fun. Write a simple play about your mood, or family, or two people arguing politics. Go to a mall or any busy public place to people watch, and assign people back stories based on their body language.

5. *Get out.* Go to a part of town you don't normally go to and have a cup of tea in the local donut joint. Watch the world of people who don't care for the biz and see if you don't get some comfort from the fact that not everyone is dying to get on a series. Most of all, leave the house. Staying home when you're low is dangerous.

6. *Save your money.* The first time you make a bundle you will want to spend some money—after all, you earned it. Go ahead once, but after that as you make more money, live like you did before you had it. Assurances are a myth in this business, so you need to save and invest (SAG offers free investment classes) and enjoy your life on the scale presented, not on the one in your head, just because you want to feel like a player. All the hype can stop as quickly as it starts—ask MC Hammer.

Being prudent about your spending and keeping your overhead manageable allows you to make better choices and have more control over your career. Even a small cushion of money gives you a clarity that lets you see the pages of a script you're working on through the lens of an artist trying to create a character rather than through the lens of the actress panicked about making the rent.

It's also a major self esteem builder when you can choose whose company you'll put yourself in based on the quality of the writing, not based on the salary they might pay you. You will be a happier, prouder artist if the money you've made holds you over to the next job.

7. *Always be polite.* With people you don't know really well, keep conversation light and positive. You never know who you are talking to, or who they'll be in years to come. Six degrees of separation would actually be a lot in this business—it's more like two or three degrees. Everyone is friends with someone. Keep your opinions about people in the business to yourself. Real conversations about your opinions concerning the value of anything involved in this business—a movie, a script, a director, or a fellow actor—should be kept for very close friends only. The telephone game is very real. A simple opinion about how bad a movie was can easily become "He hates everything about you" in a conversation with the director, without your knowing. I'm just offering this as an advisory—I'm not saying be paranoid and guard your every word.

Finally, when in doubt, say nothing. If you find yourself in a meeting or at a party of big shots, and you're unsure of what to say, be quiet and listen. You'll never be embarrassed, and most of the time people see silence as confidence, not snobbery.

I Will Do What I Have to Until I Can Do What I Want

Small tradeoffs like living in a tiny apartment or having a difficult day job until you can earn your living as an actor isn't what I'm talking about here. I'm talking about the work you do within the business. The idea that you must take acting work that you don't want, or don't feel good about, or that you will endure horrible treatment from horrible people in the business because these are all necessary in career building is a myth. The illusion is that we all have to do things we'd never do except to build a career, until we get to a place where everyone finally turns to us and says, "So now that you are a huge star, what can we do for you?"

The casting couch is the easiest illustration of this. The story goes like this.

1. In the beginning I sleep with the people who can make my career flourish.
2. It works. They get me good parts. I make it big.
3. I no longer have to trade sex for acting roles. I'm a star.

Let me present another point of view on this, because I feel this rationale is dangerous for the new artist entering the business world.

1. The things, or jobs, you do to build your career become you. You cannot do a soap opera for years and years and then have its influence magically go away when you become a big feature film actor. It all shapes you.

2. The finish line in the term "making it" is a real gray area. Every actor feels the same way about their security in this business now as they did when they started. Everyone knows it's fleeting. Certain people can feel a little less scared for their next meal, but their ego is always there telling them they have to get on with the next thing that'll keep them working and out of obscurity. This business is constantly on the lookout for the next hot prospect.

3. If you gain the reputation for doing certain things or enduring some hardship, do you really think that when you "make it" everyone is going to suddenly understand that you are no longer willing to do that thing just because you don't want to? Or do you think that having been someone that has been counted on for that behavior, that there will now be that ongoing expectation of you? I'm just trying to warn you about the false principle that every artist must be two separate people—one that has self respect and cares for their artist, and one that's a back-stabbing, anything-it-takes go-getter. It's a

big mistake to think that the two will never have to meet inside your body because you're just doing what you have to until you can do what you want. Be wary of the person that says to your face, "This is just the stuff you have to do until you get to a place where you can do what you want." They may be right about that particular instance, but be wary. It may be coming from someone who isn't concerned with your long term goals.

Roy Disney said, "Decisions are easy if you know your values." I think you have to create your habits early concerning what you will and won't tolerate from yourself and your work. Of course what comes at you will constantly challenge and change your view of what you will and won't do, but I'm saying don't think there is an automatic need to absolve yourself of your morals or standards because you are now in the biz.

A Word About Fear

There is an old Irish proverb, "Desire overcomes fear." That's true. Your days will be a bit easier if you can focus on what is at hand and let your desire take over. I was sitting on the set with David Caruso one day when a background artist asked him what it took to make it. This was his answer: "Desire. Desire is bigger than odds, it's bigger than logic. If you have desire, and you keep yourself on the playing field, it'll happen." That's succinct. He's living proof too, isn't he?

Consider my desire lesson when you're at a loss for why things aren't going in the direction you want them to. Ask yourself, "Do I have more desire than fear?" You might learn that you've been talking yourself into some reality that isn't true. You might learn that you really don't want to be on a sitcom, you really want to tour in a musical and be on stage your whole career. If TV auditions are drudgery, but learning songs for a musical is the best part of your day, learn from your desire. This is an invaluable tool for your sanity down the road.

If you try out your best ideas and fail, you learn and grow. If you try with someone else's idea in your head and fail, you learn the same lesson over and over.

Nightmares

THESE EXAMPLES ARE NOT TO scare you. They're to illustrate how far reaching the insanity of this business can be. My goal here is two-fold:

1. To anesthetize you to the madness sometimes thrown at you. By hearing about the things that have happened to me and friends of mine, hopefully you will not be shocked or thrown if something like this happens to you.

2. You'll see how little you control in the entire process. Even doing your absolute best work can sometimes take a back seat to the workings of the other people involved.

Here we go, and by the way these are all true, first hand accounts. None of this is myth or hearsay, and they are in no particular order.

I auditioned once for a casting woman who was severely hearing impaired, but she didn't tell me. During a very long "wanting a divorce" scene, I used a lot of the room. Whenever I turned away or she couldn't see my face, she'd stop reading and just stare at me. I didn't know what to do, so I'd stop too. Then the producer would nudge her with a "Go ahead!"

She'd look at her producer, and say, "What?"

"Read the line. He's ready."

The casting director would then look back at me and say, "Oh," and she'd read the next line. And so it went to its grueling finish.

The producer called my agent and angrily recounted how "cruel" I was to the casting director by purposely moving to where she could not see my mouth. "Everybody knows she can't hear!" Followed by, "We will never see your client again!"

At a network test for a TV pilot, the outcome of the discussion among the twenty-five executives in the room was that I had won the part. Then the female creator of the show spoke up, saying that the shirt I was wearing reminded her too much of her horrible ex-husband and she couldn't get beyond the image, so she could not sign off on me as the choice. The casting director, a good friend, called me directly to explain that as good as I was, to get this part I would have to return a week later, go into the same room with the same people, and do the same material in different clothing. He sheepishly mapped out the exact wardrobe I should wear so the creator would be able to "get beyond the ex-husband thing." In a room of twenty-five adults, one neurotic person had turned her "artistic process" into a therapy session and not one person in the room had the guts to say, "Come off it! We're actually going to ask this guy to come back here next week to see if he can act in different clothing?" Yes, that's how insecure they can be.

A friend called me one day and said, "I got one for the book! As I was auditioning today I watched the producer's eyes roll up and close. He fell asleep during my audition."

I met a very well-established casting director on a general meeting and as we sat down a package came for her, which she told me she had been waiting on. She then proceeded to ask me questions and look through the package. It was clear she wasn't listening. When I'd finish an answer, she'd abruptly look up and say, "Oh! Good, that sounds good." At the end of the meeting, she apologized for being distracted. When my agent asked how the meeting went, I told her. My agent called, and the casting director again apologized, but she said she liked me very much. However, I didn't get an audition call from her for five years. Casting people don't want to be reminded of their bad behavior, and if you're that reminder, your fault or not, you will not be seen.

On the eve of a premiere for a film I was in, I was called by a friend in the casting office and informed that—surprise!—a limo would pick me up and take me to the premiere! A fellow cast mate with the same first name as me, but with a smaller part, asked me if I wanted to ride with him to the premiere. I said they were sending us limos, so I'd see him there. He then called the casting director's office to discuss his limo arrangements and was informed he wouldn't be getting a limo. He launched into a tirade about playing favorites and generally insulted her.

Later that same day I called the casting director about something else entirely and she snapped at me for calling and yelling at her about the limo. Many times I tried to explain that I had no idea what she was talking about, that I hadn't called, and that since they were sending me a limo, it made no sense that I would call and yell about *not* getting one. She would not budge from her belief that she had caught me trying to call back to pretend that I never made the call. That major casting director has never called me in again for anything, ever. The final irony here is that the actor who did actually make the call is still her good friend. She has helped him many times in his career. He, of course, never bothered to clear it up on my behalf.

I was really happy to get an audition for a film being directed by a legendary director. I walked in and saw that he was busy writing something down. I said hello and waited for him to finish so I could start my reading. The casting director then smiled, letting me know this was his process, and said, "Go ahead, start." So I did. He never looked up, never stopped what he was doing, and never engaged me visually. It wasn't insulting in the end, just uncomfortable.

I sat in front of a group of men to read for their TV show when one of them told the young assistant, "Go outside and wait for lunch and bring it in the second it gets here. We're starving." He then looked at me and said, "Better read fast kid! If the food gets here before you're done, we're gonna eat!" They all laughed. Sure enough, before I finished the door burst open and lunch was presented. No one in the room spoke to or looked at me as I left.

This may be hard to believe, but again I certify this is a true story. A friend called me with the news from his agent. The news from his agent was this: "They're going to try to sneak a convicted felon rap star back in the country to star in this movie. He's been in another country hiding, to avoid his jail sentence. The news from casting was, 'If they can't get him in, the part is yours.'"

This is an illustration of how the crap comes at you from all sides when you're in the biz. A friend went to a Beverly Hills orthodontist, a doctor he didn't know, to have his teeth straightened. This Beverly Hills dentist looked over his teeth and said, "I wouldn't bother with braces with the kind of parts you'll get. The camera will never be close enough to see your teeth."

I heard the news that I would not be getting a role in a feature film that I had been very sure I was going to get after several callbacks and what felt like solid work in the room. So I called the casting director, who is a friend (don't ever do this with someone you don't *really* know), and asked him what went wrong and what more I could have done. He told me, "Nothing. I don't know if this is going to make you feel better, but the director absolutely loved you. However he also loved the other actor and he just couldn't decide, so he flipped a coin and it came up tails. You were heads."

I was auditioning for a casting director who was a very old friend. At one time we were quite close. So it was good to see him, and as we always did, we stole a little extra time to catch up before the reading. This is how it went:

Casting director: "What's new?"
Me (smiling broadly): "I'm getting married!"
Casting director: "Is she an actress?"
Me: "No."
Casting director (staring me right in the eyes): "She's a whore."

I sat there dumbfounded, staring at him and telling myself, "He didn't say what you thought he said." Then he repeated, "She's a whore." He didn't smile or laugh—his face was dead even. I hadn't moved an inch.

Then he lifted up the sides, said matter of factly, "Okay let's read this," and went on with the audition like nothing unusual had happened.

As I sat down to read for a big-budget sci-fi movie, the producer said, "I'm sorry, the director can't be here. He's dealing with a special effects emergency."

I chuckled and said, "What's that mean? You ran out of blood?" Just a funny quip, I thought.

The producer absolutely launched at me, "My husband is a serious filmmaker! Do you think its just all blood splattered everywhere and you get a good action movie! There's much more involved! To reduce it to something that simple is insulting!"

I'd been in the room for ten seconds. I had no idea what was happening. I looked to the casting director for help. He gave me a nothing-I-can-do look. I gingerly interrupted her with, "I'm not insulting your husband. I was just saying you don't hear 'special effects emergency' every day. I thought it was a funny term. That's all. You've taken this personally, and I'm sorry. It wasn't meant that way. It was an attempt at a joke, not an attack on you." She just stared daggers at me. The room was silent. I finally said, "Well, I guess this is over."

She sneered back, "Yes it is!" I got up and slinked my way out the door, feeling awful.

During a reading for a really well-written, interesting, and ultimately good independent feature film, the director stopped me and said, "Do the other character." A few lines into the other character, he said, "Stop! I was wrong, you were right. Go back to the other character." When I finished my reading he excitedly sat up, and said "Man! You're great! Are you available to do this movie?!" I never heard from him again.

My audition for an independent film (that went on to be a pretty big movie) finished with the reader asking the director, "Should we do it again? Do you want anything else?" To which the director responded, "No! That was perfect!" I never heard from them again.

In a TV pilot audition, before I read for the director (a very close friend) and the executive producer, I asked if I could read the scenes out of order. They said it was okay. After I read the first of three scenes the executive producer said, "Thank you" in the familiar tone of "That's all, good bye." I stood up and said, "Oh, okay, thanks," and left. (Usually between scenes, someone in the room will say "Great, let's do the next one" or "Next scene please," but you never hear "Thank you" until the end of the reading).

My director friend called me later saying, "What were you thinking!? You just got up and left with two other scenes to read. It was bizarre." I explained that I clearly heard the tone of dismissal in the executive producer's, "Thank you." You hear it a lot on our end. He said it wasn't true and they all sat there trying to figure out how I got so arrogant. He was embarrassed because he had bragged about me to his boss before I came in. I explained over and over that I'd never walk out in the middle of an audition unless I thought I was told to do so. A simple miscommunication, right?

My friend went back to his boss and gave him my explanation. His boss flatly denied he ever gave me any reason to leave and that no miscommunication had taken place, thereby making me just an arrogant actor who read one of three scenes, and to make some kind of statement, just got up and walked out. This director was my close friend—I'd vacationed with him and gone through the birth of his first child with him—but he stopped returning calls to me.

A friend excitedly went to shoot a part with a legendary star in a big budget movie. He checked in with the second A.D. and went to hair and make up, got his military buzz cut as required by the part, got in his uniform, and was shown to his trailer to wait. After a few hours he crept quietly on the set while they were filming to get a snack from the craft service table. He stood a moment listening and eating when he realized they were shooting his scene and someone else was saying his lines. On his approach to the set to see what was going on, he was intercepted by the second A.D., who hustled him outside and said, "The director decided to go another way." He changed out of wardrobe and went home. He got the job, was paid for the job, but was replaced on the set. This type of thing "never happens," and yet it did.

A friend who had gotten a TV show went to the fitting and was at home later when his manager and agent conference-called him, frantically asking, "What was wrong!?" He had no idea what they were talking about. The studio executives for his show had seen his wardrobe fitting Polaroids and thought he looked sad or even mad and they let his team know that if he wasn't happy with the part, they could easily replace him. This was a fitting! You put on clothes long enough to have a picture taken and then change into different clothes. It's a very mundane task that requires very little involvement. This network exec thought he could discern this actor's lack of desire for the job on his face during this routine task. My friend had to spend a fair amount of time on the phone with his team coming up with a strategy to convince the network exec that he loved his job and it was just a face he uses at fittings. He told me now he smiles as big as the sun in all the Polaroids.

A friend got a part in a pilot and went to Vancouver to shoot it. The night before they were going to start, the producer decided to have the whole cast to his room for a pre-shoot get-together. Everyone arrived in a good mood and the producer decided that it'd be fun to read the script as long as they were all there. So they did. It was great fun and the night ended with big smiles. The next day my friend's agent called him in his hotel room to say the producer was having second thoughts and was thinking of replacing him because he didn't nail it in last night's read through. He explained it wasn't a read through, they were sitting five deep on the bed just reading it and having fun. After a few calls back and forth his agent negotiated an emergency work session that day with the producer in his room if he wanted to keep his job. He did the session, acted up a storm, and kept his job. Later during the shoot, he told the producer he thought that what he had been put through was uncalled for. It was a late night, casual read through, hardly a situation where actors go all out. The producer responded "You always have to be on."

This one is so you can feel good about any blunders that might happen in agent meetings. A friend went in to meet an agent who had a sound effects machine that played applause next to his desk. When my friend would answer a question, he would get applause. He loved it. He thought it was really novel of this agent to make people feel special. So as the meeting ended my friend said, "I want to tell you I love the applause machine." The agent asked him sharply, "What applause machine?" My friend pointed to the speaker next to his desk and said, "That." The agent looked at him queerly, saying, "That's my stereo and it's playing the sounds of waves crashing on shore. There's no applause machine." My friend fell over laughing at himself—he was sure he was hearing applause! The agent was humorless about it.

A casting director told me that once during an audition an actor, trying to stress a point in the reading, kicked at the air with his foot. That action sent his backless shoe flying across the room, hitting her right in the face. Not only did she yelp from the shock of it, but it hit with enough force to make her dizzy, leaving a red mark on her face that she wore through all the other auditions that day.

I went to a preview screening of a feature film I had done. I was excited about it because I was in the trailer for the film and the trailer had been playing for weeks in theatres and on TV. I was getting lots of emails from friends saying they saw me in it. In the lobby of the theatre I shook hands and exchanged pleasantries with the director (a former actor) and producer and made my way in to find seats. The director came in and made a speech about how after this tough shoot he considered us all his family, and that he was very proud of the film. After a round of applause, the lights dimmed and the film started. I sat there anxiously as we got to my first scene. Then suddenly I went numb. I was not in the film. The people I did the scene with were in the film, but I was not. My part was in the film and my lines were being said, but not by me. No one had told me I'd been cut. As a trade courtesy, when you've been cut from a film the director usually calls you to say he couldn't use your part but it had nothing to do with your performance. I had been replaced. What made this especially shocking was seeing who they got to replace me. It was the director. He decided to reshoot my role and the do the part himself.

As funny and horrible as these stories are, you will find that everyone in the business will have the same reaction to them—open-mouthed shock that settles into

"Well, that's the business." This accepted business-wide disclaimer is the rationale for terrible treatment of people. It's also the birthplace of all the warnings you've been given about growing a thick skin. At times it feels like you are being told not to have pride or not to think you're entitled to anything better than the poor treatment that comes your way. I, of course, am going to implore you not to fall for this. You must see these events as lessons in human behavior and illustrations of how some people choose to abuse their gifts instead of making the business we all live in an easier place to be.

Remember that the biz is made up of people, and these are the choices of those people, not hard rules sent down by the heavens. Don't hate the people who do these things, blame them, or waste time waiting to get back at them. Agree to disagree. It hurts while it's happening, but get through the hurt, then settle on the fact that your pure creative spirit will not be guided into a dark place by the bad habits of those who choose negative choices over positive. And when it's your turn to run things or influence people, use your knowledge of how *not* to treat the people around you. Don't continue to use the excuse "That's the business" to cover for bad behavior.

Finding the Spirit to Go On

I sat with Adam Arkin waiting to audition one day. He chuckled to himself and said "They are in there *reading* Rip Torn. Rip Torn! This is the only business in the world where every day you get to wakeup and start all over again."

Art depends on luck and talent.

—Francis Ford Coppola

This chapter is about the long days of waiting. It is about standing around wondering if any if the seeds you planted have taken root. These are the days that fertilize the bitterness in an artist. The world needs another bitter actor like it needs another politician. Let's see if we can head you in another direction. You have to trust in your talent. I give you this to consider. Where would Billy Bob Thornton be without the effort he took to put together *Sling Blade*? Would there ever have been another role that so perfectly fit his talent as a character actor? I doubt it. He invented something special and risked a great deal getting it done. Now he's reaping the benefits of that risk. If he hadn't, he could very easily be sitting next to you at auditions. My point is this: wouldn't he still have the same talent and desire that made the Karl Childers character come alive? He's the same artist, isn't he? Aren't you also someone loaded with potential? Isn't your greatness just a risk, audition, or revelation away? It is, but this is art. There is no tangible timetable for growth or success. You must simply stay in it, so you have the chance to grow. If you let the lack of big dollar paydays inform your desire or talent, then you are doing things backwards.

The frustration of not being seen, not having anyone acknowledge this great talent that I was sure was in me, was really frustrating.

—Mark Ruffalo

Make no mistake, staying sane and focused is the hardest part of your job. The acting part is easier for you now. It should even be fun. You've trained. The acting challenges will always be exciting. It's the business side that becomes the work. You have every right to feel overwhelmed at times by the enormity of the stone you are pushing up the hill, but you should also know that the stone can reach the top every day, and that's why you should keep pushing.

Thoughts to Keep Things Straight

You are the only person who has to care about your career. The rest of the community is busy minding theirs. To endow someone else, like your agent, manager, boyfriend, parent, or teacher with the obligation of having the same fervent desire for your success is basically to encourage disappointment. Always remember that you are humbly bringing people along on your fantastic ride. You are not asking people to get so excited about you that they bring *you* along for the ride *they* want for your career.

Remember, you act because you want to. There is no outside force making you work at this. Therefore it's your job to try your best. Holding back to protect yourself from hurt or rejection is common. Make yourself uncommon.

> *Money doesn't change you, it just lets you be who you really are.*
>
> —Carrie Fisher

Learning from your failures teaches you useful lessons that you can employ to make a change. Then they are no longer failures; they are lessons.

You are not a failure if you're not on a set or stage working today. Most of the world's most brilliant actors aren't working today either.

The real skill of the business is surviving until you get the perfect job and can really fulfill yourself acting. Not every role is a perfect fit. Think of it as a parallel to finding your perfect life mate. You meet plenty of people every day, but you really connect with very few and marry only one (hopefully). This work is about exercising the creative genius within. Your challenge will be to negotiate the bog of insensitivity and land in a place where you can be as open to your artist as possible. Even jobs you get and like won't always challenge the artist within. Know that seeking the roles that best allow you to flourish and being in a healthy mental place when you get them will help you survive until gold appears in them thar hills. In case you're thinking that as an actor you should be able to flourish in any role, I ask you how many roles you watch in any week of TV viewing, and of those roles, how many speak to you and how many do you simply watch with mild interest? An actor is versatile, but surely there are limits for everyone.

They who lack talent expect things to happen without effort. They ascribe failure to a lack of inspiration or ability, or to misfortune, rather than to insufficient application. At the core of every true talent there is an awareness of the difficulties inherent in any achievement, and the confidence that by persistence and patience something worthwhile will be realized. Thus talent is a species of vigor.

—Eric Hoffer

Have a specific discussion with yourself about what you want to put into the world as an artist. Living room proclamations of "I want to be a working actor!" are too vague. You can eliminate some unemployment anxiety by being specific. You'd like to be working how? In what? With whom? Where? In the name of gaining clarity, be more specific. Ask yourself if you are not working because you've tried for roles that are perfect for you and failed to land one, or is it because you're trying the spaghetti technique where you throw any and every role up against the wall hoping that one sticks to you? If you have no real feeling for the part but feel competent to go in and use your audition chops to read well, you may end up with no job and a sadness that you're not good enough to even get the parts you don't want. Well I can tell you this: those parts don't want you either.

When we start out we chase every opportunity to get any part—student films, non-union, industrials, small theatre. That's smart. I'm not suggesting you become so picky you audition only once a month. I'm suggesting that you shouldn't feel that you lack talent if you audition for things that really don't stimulate you, and the audition doesn't yield a job or good feelings about your work. I think it's a good idea to audition a lot and improve your skill. I'm warning you about the expectation that simply by going in on a hundred things, you should end up with a job. Not if the hundred things are things that you aren't willing to admit aren't right you. When the words don't stimulate your artist in any way, you're trying to undo your training for the sake of a salary. We are human, and we have the tolerances and intolerances that we have. Money has a way of making every job feel like a perfect fit, but did the words and ideas on the page thrill you? Consider this thought before you allow the depression of "I suck!" to set in. This isn't permission to have sour grapes. This is being clear with your goals and knowing your strengths as an actor before you settle on the idea that "no matter what you go in for, no one will hire you!" How far do you think a young Bob Dylan would get on *American Idol*?

In the acting world you have to keep in mind that money has no bearing on talent. This quote is from entrepreneur Ken Hakuta, but I like its sentiment: "Lack of money is no obstacle. Lack of an idea is an obstacle."

> *Nothing in this world can take the place of persistence. Talent will not; nothing is more common than unsuccessful people with talent. Genius will not; unrewarded genius is almost a proverb.*
>
> —Calvin Coolidge

There may be days when you sit and sift through your mind for an answer on how to turn this stagnant period around so you can go out today and get a job. You're feeling that all your effort has been in vain, so now you're willing to "give in to the way the game is played." You'll try anything. You're tired of being a maverick and tired of hearing no. Your head will fill with all the "good" advice you've gotten from any and every source in your travels, and your insecurity is now telling you that the advice must be right. Logic dictates that if your approach was right, you'd be working. So you decide you're going to make changes. Be very careful here. That loud voice that's screaming for attention is the voice that needs a quick fix so the pain of unemployment can go away, if only for a day. Your artist's instinct will tell you what you must change in yourself to grow. Use these days to have a very frank talk with your inner artist about changes to make, if any, and realize that these feelings connect you with the consciousness of every artist out there. Every artist suffers.

This is also when taking a path already trodden starts to look good. Unlike in the banking world, it doesn't really work that way. The greatness of acting and the arts is that many different paths can lead to the same place. Being on someone else's path won't land you where it landed them, and I'll wager it won't land you where you want to be either. Making your own path is generally the only way to go about it. So have faith in the fact that your path is on course. Results are an easy way to rate your path. They may not be what you want right now, but if you look at your progress on the whole, you'll probably see a strong path toward the goal. Gore Vidal said, "Style is knowing who you are, what you want to say, and not giving a damn."

In the Meantime

The killer of all good artists is *the meantime*. This is the time we are doing anything but standing on stage or in front of the camera. We have a bad habit of calling anything but work down time.

I have already made the suggestion that you get some other real thing to do. This is where that idea picks up. Wouldn't it be great to never have to feel that you're dealing with the meantime? Wouldn't it be nice to have a job or endeavor that will give you some distraction and fulfillment?

How do you know when it's time to find this other thing? When you have thoughts like:

I've made a big career mistake.

It's so much easier for other actors.

This should be easier to accomplish.

Everyone else is working but me.

Every other actor is taken seriously, but I'm not.

The whole town loves him or her, but not me.

If I had his money (looks, connections, etc.) it'd be that easy for me too.

If they gave me thirty takes and an editor I could do that too.

If I got a lobotomy I could be that mediocre too.

What you are doing is allowing the meantime to turn the business uncontrollables into controllables. Your frustration turns into criticism of others. The plan here is to focus on what you can do and leave alone what you can't. You can't really know why anyone is chosen for a job, so you have to let it go. Keep your energy focused on things you can accomplish. Accomplishing the play reading or the painting of your apartment will encourage you to keep getting things done. Sitting idle and stewing is a very easy thing to fall into. It's easy to say, "What more can I do? The phone has to do its job now." But there are always things in your life that need doing; go do them. Bring a fuller life to each audition. Don't just bring the actor in search of stardom.

Life is what happens while you are busy making other plans.

—John Lennon

The meantime can be a very potent time for you. Don't waste it watching TV and complaining about your agent or your lack of an agent. Use it to remind yourself that you have one of the best jobs in the world. You get to create every day.

There will be days when you feel like there is a large stop sign posted right outside your front door to remind you that you don't belong in the club and no matter how hard you try, you won't succeed. It's not true, but it can feel that way.

Many of life's failures are people who did not realize how close they were to success when they gave up.

—Thomas A. Edison

The Beauty of the Business

Your whole life could change in a moment. The phone could ring, and everything you've suffered up to now could be gone. It's the magic of the journey. It's one of the businesses where your whole career can be made in a day or a week or a month. It's that quick. So keep the faith that even if you can't see any light today, you have no idea what's working at the zillion meetings that go on every day in offices where people are trying to make shows and movies that will need you. It's endless, because entertainment is now America's biggest export.

In Summary

NO ONE TOLD ME ANY OF THE things I've shared with you in this book when I started out. I was handed the time-proven, three-chapter manual—how tough it is, how tough it's going to be, and how taking everyone's crap until you've "made it" is all you can look forward to. No one jumps into any endeavor and knows everything they should know the first day, month, or year. The learning curve is part of the journey, and the early days are usually the fun days when you look back on them. It's your Wild West! Deepening your awareness as well as your acting chops is very smart.

I hope you will use the thoughts from this book to make the seemingly impossible become feasible and to set yourself on a course of good habits with less anxiety about the unknown. Fear can be a tool or an inhibitor; it's up to you to make it the former.

I also know it's lonely being in this business without a good mentor or support system. I hope this book has filled some of that gap for you, if even in a simple way. Moreover, I hope it has taught you that building a support system is paramount to your success and sanity. Find those people who are good to you and support them even if they're your "competition," and see if what goes around doesn't come around.

If you get confused, read this book again. When you get a job and feel great, pay it forward. Make your days about creating a place for your artist to thrive. By seeing the lunacy of this business not as lunacy, but simply as the way the business is currently conducted, your days will make sense and you won't be knocked off balance.

Finally, don't fear being swallowed by the monster and becoming shallow and insincere. You won't lose what you brought to the game unless you want to. Fear, instead, not showing the planet your level best, your genius, your spirit. As I said before, your true self is all you have to offer, and that's a fact. If you offer it with the enthusiasm of an artist, you will be fulfilled and happy. If you offer it with conditions of fame and money, you might get rich, but I honestly question whether you'll be happy. Both are certainly possible. I have just known a lot of successful actors who remain dependent on the media's response to their work for their happiness.

It is my firm belief that only art can save the world. Go forward and make change.

About the Author

Markus Flanagan has never needed to hold a day job throughout his twenty-year acting career. Right out of acting school he starred in *Biloxi Blues* alongside Matthew Broderick, and his first TV pilot audition landed him a series with George Clooney. He's starred in three prime-time series, made fifty guest TV show appearances, and acted in ten feature films, five stage plays, and five movies of the week. He learned many valuable lessons from observing the successes and mistakes of those he's worked with, including Mike Nichols, Aidan Quinn, Tom Cruise, Jerry Hall, Christopher Walken, Stockard Channing, Tyne Daly, Michael Madsen, Jerry Seinfeld, Tim Allen, Kirstie Alley, the Olsen Twins, and many more.

He's written five plays, all of which have been produced in Los Angeles and Santa Fe, NM, and he has sold a screenplay to Fox. He directed the TV show *Unfabulous*, and is the creator of the LA Café Plays play series that continues to be a great success in Santa Monica. He lives and teaches acting in Los Angeles.

Please visit his website, onelessbitteractor.com, for more information.

Sentient Publications, LLC publishes books on cultural creativity, experimental education, transformative spirituality, holistic health, new science, ecology, and other topics, approached from an integral viewpoint. Our authors are intensely interested in exploring the nature of life from fresh perspectives, addressing life's great questions, and fostering the full expression of the human potential. Sentient Publications' books arise from the spirit of inquiry and the richness of the inherent dialogue between writer and reader.

Our Culture Tools series is designed to give social catalyzers and cultural entrepreneurs the essential information, technology, and inspiration to forge a sustainable, creative, and compassionate world.

We are very interested in hearing from our readers. To direct suggestions or comments to us, or to be added to our mailing list, please contact:

SENTIENT PUBLICATIONS, LLC

1113 Spruce Street

Boulder, CO 80302

303-443-2188

contact@sentientpublications.com

www.sentientpublications.com